BAD MOUTH

ABOUT
QUANTUM
BOOKS

QUANTUM, THE UNIT OF
EMITTED ENERGY. A QUANTUM
BOOK IS A SHORT STUDY
DISTINCTIVE FOR THE AUTHOR'S
ABILITY TO OFFER A RICHNESS OF
DETAIL AND INSIGHT WITHIN
ABOUT ONE HUNDRED PAGES
OF PRINT. SHORT ENOUGH TO BE
READ IN AN EVENING AND
SIGNIFICANT ENOUGH
TO BE A BOOK.

Robert M. Adams

BAD MOUTH

Fugitive Papers on the Dark Side

University of California Press

Berkeley • Los Angeles • London

University of California Press
Berkeley and Los Angeles, California

University of California Press, Ltd.
London, England

Copyright © 1977 by
The Regents of the University of California

ISBN 0-520-03381-7
Library of Congress Catalog Card Number: 76-50241
Printed in the United States of America

1 2 3 4 5 6 7 8 9

*Language was given to man
to conceal his thoughts.*

SAINT RÉAL, TALLEYRAND, OR STENDHAL

*Ideas were given to man
to prevent him from thinking.*

the PSEUDO–TERTULLIAN

Contents

Preface

Though the studies making up this little collection were not written to fit any particular schema—growing, rather, as a set of free variations on a gradually emerging theme—they do in fact form a pattern of sorts. The first two focus on the idea of counter-language, language used to hinder people or hurt them in a variety of symbolic and practical ways, mostly quite familiar. The next two are concerned with language that deliberately violates standards of decency and standards of truth (such as survive); emphasizing the general prevalence of such language, they look into the consequences of its no longer being exceptional. The last two pieces, departing from a direct concern with language, devote themselves to what I sense as a new and autonomous status for the ugly in modern life, and with the frequent metaphors of rags, garbage, and excrement in which that ugliness finds expression.

If the successive essays do not display, at least they suggest, a wide range in the negative and hostile uses of language, both everyday and artistic, from light and occasional personal insult to total alienation from a culture and all its works. Implicit in the arrangement is a specific historical thesis, which I haven't tried to emphasize but feel obliged to declare explicitly here. I think a big balance has shifted recently, say within the last fifty years. The lacerating and deliberately offensive mode in art and literature, which used to be very much a minority mode, very much an occasional and subordinate effect within a larger composition, is now predominant. Varieties of complicity and mutual accommodation between writer and reader or artist and viewer, which though tacit used to be widespread if not universal, are now largely obsolete.

The causes of this immense change, like its full consequences, are not beyond speculation, but they are not the particular concern of a cultural commentator. Quite possibly the world is deteriorating at an unprecedented clip; what used to be exceptional iniquity is now commonplace, and the disciplines of art and literature must strain their foulest resources to keep up with the realities of our precipitous slide into the abyss. Or, alternatively, the world is very much what it always was, but old commonplaces and artistic conventions have been exhausted, fashion requires something new, so artists and writers cast about for the nearest taboo to violate. Perhaps we should see the contemporary vogue for black humor, macabre sensationalism, and sordid fecality as the opening up of a more forceful and expressive vocabulary for the imagination. Perhaps we should see in it only the cultivation of short-term shock-effects. Very likely it has something to do with the destruction (at least in their own self-definitions) of old artistic and literary elites, the advent (for good, for evil, for inevitable) of audiences trained on comic books, television, and the movies. In any event, I am neither documenting nor describing here what I sense as a vast change in the cultural weather, far less explaining it, but simply assuming its existence as a background for some specifics.

When one's subject is so sweeping, there's no reason to be nice in the selection of examples: a random sampling across the board will serve the purpose of suggestion as well as any close arrangement of hard evidence, supposing such were available. Though I talk now of popular and now of literary usage, sometimes of formal art and sometimes of those loose habits known as folkways, the central interest of the study is nothing but vocabulary. By that I mean simply the repertoire of devices available to express or repress, divert or disguise, what for shorthand's sake we can call our nasty, authentic "selves." If there's been a change in the cultural weather, it should show in our constitutive vocabulary; and if it shows in that vocabulary, it won't be long in altering our definitions of "self." So far as I have a thesis, it can be cast in the form of a premise and an open-ended question: The art of modern living is the art of washing clean in dirty water; but if the language with which we measure clean and dirty is itself in question—what then?

The subject may well be topical, as I think, but topicality is only an excuse, not a reason, for venturing down so dark a path. These are high-energy topics, and refract through different personalities in diverse and revealing ways. There are sunlit personalities to whom the very thought of sitting down deliberately to discuss the vindictive and the repugnant will be, not so much disagreeable, as incomprehensible and strange. Others will find the idea of talking decorously about ways of fracturing the decorums to be evasive and effete in itself. I cannot pretend to be of one mind about my own venture. Destructive uses of language, fantasies of filth and horror and hatred, are deeply rooted in the instinctual nature, perhaps not of everybody, but of many of us; yet I doubt if there's much to glory about in that fact. There's no exorcising one's fate in having been born to a black imagination, a cutting tongue, and an instinct for bleak landscapes; but history at her kindest sometimes grants one a perspective and with it a sense of communal rather than individual misfortune, such as passes in certain circles for comfort.

In the course of turning and re-turning these nasty topics, I have acquired just enough experience with reactions to feel confident that few are unrevealing, none are universally persuasive, and the most interesting are sometimes the least coherent. Anyone who talks about the way we talk can't help becoming part of his own subject. Sometimes this puts one in the position of trying to open the refrigerator door fast enough to see if the light really goes off when it's shut. So much self-questioning may distress readers who have come to the book expecting to be told what to think about the subject. I'm afraid it cannot be helped; the theme is corrosive, and can't be handed round in paper cups. The most one can hope is that laying out some intuitions about it will be provocative as well as pro-voking.

Of the essays that follow, "Dirty Stuff" appeared in *Columbia Forum* for Summer, 1973, "Ideas of Ugly" and "Rags, Garbage, and Fantasy" in *Hudson Review* for Spring, 1974 and Spring, 1976. "Ugly" has been sub-stantially rewritten for this collection, the other two revised less drastically. I am grateful to the editors for permission to reprint.

Santa Fe, New Mexico   R. M. A.
7 December, 1976

We have met the enemy, and he is us.
–*Pogo*

Bad Mouth and
Other Second Games

"Bad mouth" in its pure original is an active transitive verb with the odor of the ghetto upon it, and a meaning akin to "denigrate." It's a relatively new term, not yet enrolled in any of the standard compendia of slang,* though it has a kissing cousin in the predominantly southern expression "poor mouth," which, however, implies self-deprecation. "Bad mouth" is a black term primarily; but it is an exception to the common black reversal of the term "bad" (whereby, for example, a "bad nigger" is a good brother, and a pair of particularly jazzy shoes in an Oakland shoestore will be advertised, simply but eloquently, as "Bad").

*An exception to be made here for Clarence Major's *Dictionary of Afro-American Slang* (International Publishers, 1970); and there may be more recent compendia that have escaped my notice.

Another peculiar feature of the locution is its directness. You don't talk evilly *about* your victim, you lay it on him, you put him down, you bad mouth him. No niceties or secondary implications attach to it. To libel someone is a rather elaborate process: it is to publish formally before a significant public some item of derogatory information that one knows, or has reason to know, is untruthful—the fine print of the statute contains a lot more, but in mercy I forbear. Bad-mouthing has no such peripheral qualifications; it amounts to nothing more than vocal hostility, but it is hostility directed immediately against the victim. Like that primitive satire of which we've heard so much, it is a malevolent and rancorous action, perhaps containing overtones of hex and whammy. It is an evil verbal sign; it is not so much satire (which holds up to disapproval) as invective (which is symbolic or actual harm). It may be shouted, spoken conversationally, or grumbled under the breath; it may be face to face or behind the back. I'm not at all sure that bad mouth can be written—that seems like stretching the boundaries of the concept—and I'm quite sure it rarely occurs in the passive: you can't easily *be* bad-mouthed, you bad-mouth somebody else.

A particular and frequent application of bad mouth occurs in sports, where it provides a poor man's counterpart to what more uppity circles call "gamesmanship." Mute ferocity is the traditional posture of the muscle-man, exemplified in the scowling game-face with its clenched jaw; but talking and taunting are sometimes of useful local application. Football line-men who come to intimate push and grunt with par-ticular opponents over and over again in the course of a game can hardly avoid conversation, and obviously don't choose neutral or abstract topics on which to discourse. Before and even during a boxfight, some pugs (of whom Muhammad Ali comes immediately to mind) enjoy bad-mouthing their opponents—though I think they find it safe to talk in the ring mainly during clinches, or when dealing with an overmatched oppo-nent. An open mouth may get busted more easily than one that's clenched shut. But the talk often serves clas-sic ends—to nerve the talker, to discourage or terrify the man addressed. And there's always a lively possi-bility that prefight bluster is mimic menace, per-formed for publicity reasons.

In any event, fighting and football, as violent contact sports, don't lend themselves during the contest itself to speech much more articulate than grunting, or occa-sional yelping. The tongue busies itself chiefly in the intervals when the heavier muscles aren't occupied, so the talking, such as it is, doesn't really become part of the game. On the other hand, concentration-sports like baseball, golf, tennis, and basketball often use bad-mouthing as an integral part of the game itself, or rather as an adjunct anti-game. For example, baseball coaches and the reserves on the bench are expected to join with the players on the field in maintaining a stream of "chatter." The uneasy thought obtrudes that some of this noise may be necessary because the game's so slow: if an infielder is hollering something, there's at least a chance he isn't asleep. But the chatter often aims specifically to break a pitcher's control, a batter's self-confidence, or a base-runner's attention. It is a deliberate provocation. Some catchers are reputed to have had a special knack for saying unnerving things to batters as they advanced toward the plate. Some pitchers talk, or affect to talk, to the ball before they throw it—as if putting special energies and erratic intentions into it that will enable it to dodge the hitter's bat. The act suggests deep concentration, secrecy, and a hidden complicity with the inanimate world from which the batter is excluded.

Most of all, basketball players, who pair off in the course of a game and thus spend a good deal of time in the company of a specific opponent, have a particular habit of bad-mouthing the fellow they're yoked with for the evening. Mr. Tommy Curtis, who played guard for UCLA a couple of years ago, had a fine, natural flow of language, and made it a major part of his game to bother his man by putting him down verbally. Whatever might upset, unbalance, or distract the man could be counted on to find its way onto Tommy's tireless tongue. Sometimes the stream of provocation irritated a victim into playing better than he otherwise would have; on balance, it bothered more opponents than it stimulated, essentially because it forced them to play two games at once, only one of which they were good at. If he tried to answer back, the opponent was dead—overwhelmed, out of it.

Even to say nothing at all in answer to Tommy Curtis required a major effort; putting out of your mind his cocky, derisive, irritating chatter was practically impossible. He was not, in the classic phrase, Actually Cheating; the rules of basketball place no limits on the activity of the mouth, except when disputing officials. Tommy was fulfilling a significant function of language, which is to mislead and distract attention, to inflict a stutter on the actor's single-minded coordination. In the magician's patter, this function is primary and accepted; in most games, we consider it exceptional and a little shady; in life at large, it has many applications, involving many varieties of teasing, distraction, and provocation besides direct insult.

Considered simply as a variant form of insult, bad-mouthing an opponent doesn't ordinarily rise to high art; intricate, imaginative abuse is not to be expected under the circumstances. The usual pattern is for the artist to pick on a feature of the victim's person or performance, and then nag him. If he misses a shot badly, throws the ball away, or commits a silly foul, he's not to be allowed to forget it. He can be shouted at, derided, teased for things he said before the game or in another context. His mannerisms can be dissected unmercifully; the powers of grotesque metaphor are unleashed against him. A successful job of bad-mouthing imposes on the victim a new definition of the game, unfavorable possibly to him and surely to his team. He is already in a competitive, a stimulus-situation, and matched against an opponent whom he can easily be led to oppose one-on-one. The bad-mouther invites him to forget the other eight men on the court, and concentrate on getting back at the invidious voice that's lacerating him. In the personal contest that bad mouth stimulates either player may win or lose, but he who gets most involved in it is in danger of neglecting the team play that most directly determines the final score.

Thus direct personal insult is only the upper register of a larger duplicity that's involved in making one's opponent unexpectedly play two games at once, or a second instead of a first. Even with a minimum of speech, the simple acts of interruption, distraction, erratic timing, and irrelevant impulse may be acts of disconcerting aggression against an opponent and his game. In a tense situation, any airy, idle gesture, whether verbal or otherwise, may be an assault on the nerves. One thinks of the protracted silent pause before a golf putt, and the awful temptation to break it. Even outside direct game situations, breaking a man's concentration may be a way of breaking him. Talkative torturers, like chatty M'sieu Pierre in Nabokov's *Invitation to a Beheading,* deliberately add the agony of irrelevant and silly conversation to the sinister pressure of behaving well in the face of imminent decapitation. Porfiry Petrovich plays much the same game with Raskolnikov in *Crime and Punishment.* Distortions imposed on the act of speech itself may also be upsetting. Doubletalk, in the days when that game was comically fashionable, consisted of using just enough semi-familiar vocables to make a discourse seem sensible, mixed with just enough nonsense-syllables to make its total import undecipherable. It tantalized, inviting and frustrating with the same gesture, like its original, the Jabberwocky speech of *Through the Looking Glass*. Lesislative filibusters, in which the delaying orator goes far out of his way to say as little as possible, in which the parliamentary forms are meticulously observed while the actual content of the speech is made offensively minimal, provide another known instance of language used for impedance and interdiction. Some academic departments are known to have a fixed quota of quibbling and bickering which they are bound to expend in every meeting, regardless of the subject. Under these circumstances, shrewd managers give trivial matters first place on the agenda, so that the itch for debate may be exercised on them, while significant business, saved for the last weary ten minutes of the meeting, is passed in a rush. Even ordinary social intercourse provides examples of language used to suppress, rather than express, ideas. The high-pressure talker pours forth an unbroken stream of irrelevant detail, not out of an urge to say something, but to prevent something, anything, else from being said. It's preemptive or diversionary language, growing as often as not out of unexpressed anxiety. A more obvious example of the same thing is the encounter of two people who are jointly determined to avoid an embarrassing topic; the "made" conversation with which they fill the air usually takes the form of collusion, not attack, but it serves the classic purpose of a second game, preventing recognition of the first. For the hostile element to emerge, the balance of forces need alter only a little, as when one person wants to tease or take advantage of the other by feinting toward the taboo topic.

Almost by definition, speech entertaining a covertly antagonist relation between agent and object involves a second game in the form of a putdown. The lecturer who stresses his contacts in Washington, his badges of honor, his intimacy with the great or presumed great, is letting his second game triumph over the first—just like the student who cites Wittgenstein or Todorov in support of a resonant commonplace. Literary allusion has sometimes become a private-key game, entitling the knowing reader to share a smirk of recognition with the knowing author, excluding those wretches who don't have the key in advance. I have known participants in panel-discussions who, while ostensibly trying to contribute to the topic, were really busy making their names known to the audience: "'Bulkington,' the President said to me just the other day, 'BULKINGTON,' he said, 'there's just one thing we've got to do about this matter.'" But here we verge on the variety of literary duplicity much in evidence lately under the rubric of "bad faith," most in evidence when the writer tries to dramatize, by talking about his bad faith, his desire not to be in that interesting condition.

Overt and explicit literary trickery is a variant and perhaps a more interesting response to the experience of bad faith; and Henrik Ibsen exemplifies it with his special version of the second game which could be called "bait-and-switch." His middle plays regularly engage the reader in a contest of appearances fought out between the characters. To the "reality" of this contest the viewer is forced to commit himself; in the playhouse, he has no other reality to set against what the stage gives him. But no sooner has he committed himself than the whole action is denounced as a fraud and a deception. A mere tissue of appearances, that is what a stage play inherently is, and when the character Nora Helmer denounces her husband, and behind him the audience, for condemning her to an existence of appearances, she's blaming them for being an audience at a stage play in which she is an actress. Ever since Baudelaire blamed his bored reader for seeking vicarious stimulation in his verses, that second game of attacking the reader as a vampire has underlain (at least potentially) the first one of attracting him as a client. Even without the ethical overtone, writers like Barth and Borges continually play the bait-and-switch, which in essence is no more complicated than luring the reader onto a narrative carpet and then yanking it out, more or less violently, from underneath him. Second game may not characterize all literature, but much of it conceals deliberately as it reveals; we do not know for sure what second game Homer was playing when he took time out in the middle of the *Iliad* to describe the shield of Achilles, but he surely had one in mind. The detective story, like the symbolist poem, uses two sets of energies, positive and negative; it is a "pattern to make." Given an ostensible arrangement of particulars with some anomalies or deficiences in it, the reader is challenged to remake it, using the known as a basis to guess at the unknown. Riddles, runes, charades, emblems, allegories, rebuses, and heraldic insignia all involve an arrangement of hints and reticences, the first game of assertion complicated by the second one of withholding. Catechisms, starting from known answers, devise more or less difficult questions to trigger the appropriate responses. For each yang in these patterns there's an inevitable yin; they are isometric verbal exercises, built to an instability that requires intervention by the interpreter.

So far, we've ignored the many ways in which a player of verbal games may be trying to act on himself quite as much as on his opponent; but it's often a function of linguistic aggression to exercise pseudo-courage (or, for that matter, pseudo-desire) as a surrogate for the genuine article. Animals yelp at an enemy they don't dare attack; or sometimes, by a process of yelping, yelling, and bristling, they build themselves up for an encounter. False courage builds true, as men write sonnets to prove they are in love, or to talk themselves into being in love, or to postpone doing something about it. Threats, boasts, and bluffs, rising to spread-eagle oratory and chauvinistic epithets, serve similar contradictory functions; like a cat's bristling and arching her back, they try to obviate conflict by scaring off an enemy, but prepare for it at the same time. In the Japanese martial arts, offensive gestures are accompanied by lots of shouting; even weight-lifters as they snatch and hoist their vast, inanimate burdens, encourage themselves with yelps and howls. Menace, specific or generic, is an art in itself, one of whose conventions is that real power lurks behind a quiet verbal front. "The cheaper the crook, the gaudier the patter," says Sam Spade contemptuously; his own patter, severe but vivid, is an authentic Senecan rebuke to lesser rhetorics. A good menace has always a dead quality about it; what's implicit is that we've played this scene before. Argot, thieves' jargon, and the showbiz lingo of carnies, all private languages of outlaw-groups, are commonly explained as the result of a need for secret communication; but as they advertise membership in a gang of hardened pros, they carry tacit connotations of menace. Very likely they are used for the second purpose as much as for the first, and sometimes to reassure the members of the wicked gang that even when they are not doing wicked things, they are still members of a wicked gang. Poets, sometimes, when they are not actually writing their poems, feel the need for similar reassurance that they are still poets.

It's an old story, of course, that self-definition is only a little patch of that network of promises and taboos, directives, conditionings, and associations by which we are guided, for better or worse, in shaping and socializing our raw libidos. In a large way, language itself, and the whole symbol-making, surrogate-using, indirection-pursuing part of our being constitute second games against instinctive response—a round-about imposed on a process which for animals is simpler but not wholly simple. The giant systems of conditioning and punishment required to maintain the round-about testify in themselves to its "unnaturalness"—using that word in the most primitivistic of its senses. But there's a softer and more private side to the second game of language; it is the undervoice of murmured speech that each of us carries with him as a constant intimate companion. The things one says to oneself while performing an absorbing physical task are a tangle of admonitions, incitements, ejaculations, exorcisms, and nameless intimacies, delivered through a multiplicity of voices. One says certain things to drive them out of the mind, one repeats nonsense syllables ("so, so, so, too, too, too") to keep ideas from forming in the mind, one grunts and says "Now, then," one hums or lilts under one's breath, one curses the work or the tool or oneself, one asks rhetorical questions and breaks off sentences in mid-phrase. Speech-bits and fragments rise out of the past, are chewed for a moment to get their flavor, and spat out. All this helter-skelter activity of mind and throat and tongue surrounds the quiet and purposeful labor of the hands, as if to protect it, to silence and distract inner voices that are really extraneous to the work. Placating, suppressing, and diverting impulses that lie below the level of language (*hysterica passio,* terror of the *gouffre,* the mere restless, bubbling motion of the mind—all verbal formulations of subverbal impulses, and so bound to be vague), these are major psychic functions of word-play. Voltaire said if he had not been a writer, he would have murdered: happy the man who can thus convert his vice into his profession. Meanwhile, the least ferocious of us pass through life, cushioned on a constant inner dialogue of one, the voice at our inner ear forever prompting, teasing, warning, reminding, and comforting us. An arch-actor, it will readily admit to being our inner self when we challenge it; but as occasion demands, it can instantly become, and without the slightest warning, whatever other mask's mouth seems opportune, whether God, society, morality, the law, a leering goatfoot, a winsome nymph, or a potbellied Silenus.

Our repertoire of double games is inexhaustible. As we talk a man out of shooting a basketball or hitting a tennis stroke, we talk our friends away from awkward topics, talk our enemies or our colleagues to death, talk ourselves into a creative verbal cocoon of passive, rhythmic sensitivity. All the linguistic duplicities of literary artists (who for thousands of years have kept mental reservations for patterns while maintaining a public pretense of earnestly and simple-mindedly asserting) are mere tidal pools and tricklets by the great ocean of public tergiversation and duplicity, a simpler name for which is lying. So far as it isn't simply brute misstatement of facts, the classic aim of this exercise is to arrange a set of individual truths to produce an impression that's totally false. *Suppressio veri* and *commis-*

sio falsi are the Gog and Magog of existence in human
society: a thinking man can only marvel that no day
passes without a thousand solemn idiots swearing publicly to tell "the truth, the whole truth, and nothing but
the truth"—as if the whole truth could ever be told,
given matters of the least complexity, under a
thousand volumes. Even to protest the difficulty of
truth is to betray it; for one's protest implies special
exalted standards, and there's no one of us who doesn't
live snugly enough in the enseamed, sweaty security of
a thousand prudent, approximate lies. Even truth can
be a lie when social context decrees that simple truth is
not to be spoken. "You tell me you're going to Minsk
so I'll think you're going to Pinsk; but I happen to
know that you *are* going to Minsk, so why do you lie
to me?" Such are the second games that language can
be made to play even against itself. And all this mold-
ing and management of meaning in or against context
is simply an exaggeration of what the linguistically-
conditioned mind does all the time, in the course of
compressing, combining, sorting, and packaging
bundles of blurred sensation into handy conceptual
units. This great rummage and bustle takes place in
that dark and silent shipping-and-receiving room of
the head, where nerve roots feed into the brain—and
where, in the interests of economy and order, a vast
amount of perception is subordinated, classified and
rejected, in order to suit the preconceptions of the
mind. The mind's war against perception is as fierce as
its struggle against new and "upsetting" ideas; com-

forting words and familiar concepts are its best weapons in this sometimes-too-successful war. For all the odds favor the defense. We don't perceive anything without stylizing it; we don't have anything to correct our stylizings with except our perceptions, which are themselves already stylized. The mind's circle is not quite closed, but we struggle against odds to keep it a little open, and every "success" closes our mind a little to the quarter from which our next defeat will arrive.

Apart from other considerations, language makes a marvellously comfortable nest for the mind, far downier than anything the rude empirical world can provide. In a famous passage, Montaigne speaks feelingly of ignorance as a soft and pleasant pillow on which to rest a prudent head, but he had never seen a Marxist cradled in the arms of what he pleased to call the dialectic. Ideologies and their arcane vocabularies are second games that can triumph all too completely even in the most intimate forum of the mind; and language-people when they form a class (an intelligentsiya) are chiefly of social value as they prevent ugly facts from being seen, nasty questions from being asked, the verbal mask from being cracked.

First games are rarer every way, and harder to identify than second. The games we play by habit and instinct, and to which we feel language is a sort of counter, are themselves symbolic equivalents of more brutal and savage games planted within us long before language took root on our tongue, or games as such were initiated in our culture. It its first stages, which each of us must recapitulate, life is agony or bliss, torture or ecstasy. To the beat of these gigantic hammers—hunger, lust, fear, pain—our being is shaped, as is the being of every other infant animal. Language is part of the social machinery with which we smother that ferocious tattoo, or soften it to manageable tonalities—perhaps mute it altogether. A man who has achieved unusual success in this line we commonly refer to as a stuffed shirt: what he has killed within him is the foolish, passionate world of the instincts. Thus it's by a curious confusion, as it seems to me, that some revisionist Freudians have lately tried to substitute language for libido as a basic determinant of behavior, making the second game not only an index of the first, but a handle by which it can be manipulated. A nexus between language and libido there doubtless is, but surely the areas have a measure of autonomy and are linked only loosely and secondarily by for-the-most-part culturally determined bonds. What develops late as part of the deformation-structure that forms the problem can hardly be converted into its solution. Most of the words that make us so unhappy we don't even know till after the giant battles of hunger and jealousy, lust and rage and excrement, have been fought—battles all the more titanic (psychically speaking) because the central participant is himself so tiny, so focussed on his own furious appetites. Even our physiology tells the same story: the language-and-abstraction functions of the upper brain are imposed upon and develop later than the automatic and instinctive centers of the lower brain.

But the reduction of the arts to philology is in the air these days, and to work on this assumption is very much the in thing. To be sure, there's a range of truths to be discovered on the premise that the message is in fact its medium, that the language we use controls what we think we want to express. Being new and fashionable, the approach is being pushed for all it's worth, and then some. Philosophers are all into the language of propositions and proposition-makers, literary critics assume that particular linguistic usages not only shape decisively, but *are* the significant insights of poets, while social scientists tend to see language patterns as controlling, defining, and in fact constituting essential behavior. The linguistic key does actually work, to a degree, too, as did previous keys of economic and libidinal determinism—to a degree. Then as now, the degree depended largely on the subtlety and flexibility of the mind manipulating the key, and on the careful selection of locks on which to exercise one's chosen instrument. Language controls thought and channels feeling, even feeling so deep we're tempted to call it instinct, but controls in so many different ways—yielding here, impeding there, subverting and colluding simultaneously—that any one formula of relatedness is sure to be misleading. To manage the key successfully calls for such an array of skills and such a measure of cooperation that it's likely more practical just to think of it as a doorknocker that may or may not get a response.

Actually, the more elaborate our theories of language, the more social and psychic weight we put on the act of speech, the less natural play we're likely to allow ourselves in common—and it is common, common as dirt—palaver. Musical training consists very largely in getting out of the conscious mind and into the fingers or into the vocal cords those intricate coordinations that music demands. Even "simple" speech is so far from simple that it calls for multiple coordination between more elements of our organism than one could readily enumerate; and a whole complex of speech disorders shows how easy it is to overload or disorder the delicate process. If we all thought as carefully as they do over the full consequences of our words, we should all wind up sounding like Philadelphia lawyers: even as it is, a modicum of effort often makes for a choked and garbled prose style—as any reader of student papers will testify. This isn't an argument for loose and careless speech, though I confess to a faith that some pretty heavy thought—as long as it's lucid—can be put into buoyant packages. In any event, it's a pretty horrifying prospect that we might be asked to lay on our linguistic habits the same therapeutic burden that solemn, simple-minded Freudians sometimes place on what they call, artlessly, "genital satisfaction." Eisenhower-syntax would then be an ailment as richly symptomatic as impotence is today, and vocabulary-enlargement would replace sex-therapy. But why indeed should we think that the way to play successfully one game or set of games is to transform it into another? Though the world's many games often interfere with one another, the wise mind will recognize that there really isn't any one master-game that makes us automatically successful in all the rest. We play at them as they present themselves—win a few, lose a few—and count ourselves lucky if Tommy McFate Curtis doesn't pop up and force us to play two at once when we came to the court expecting to play only one. When that does happen, it may well strike us as unfair; on the other hand, it's probably more fair, and certainly more interesting, than if all games were at bottom only one game. Even as it is, there are times when basketball players seem less interested in playing basketball than in playing the rules of basketball—which is a very different game indeed.

This whole discussion has implied, if not stated, an anti-verbal invidium, but something serious should be said in praise of the superficiality and speciousness that language makes possible. As they approach or try to recover from crises of action, societies like individuals seem to need superficial, simplistic philosophies which combine a lot of language with very few ideas. Endless verbalizing preceded the Puritan outburst of 1640, and after the issues were exhausted if not settled, it required the deliberately superficial philosophy of a Shaftesbury to paper them over. In our own day, it's a particular function of language to shield us as best it can from the intolerable glare of Nothing and Nonbeing. Beckett, for example, hangs out for us a wordscreen of terrible fragility and banality, which is always threatening to split apart and so reveal something inconceivably awful—perhaps the world as it really is or more likely as it really is not. As atmospheric gasses soften the otherwise intolerable rays of the sun, so the gasses of language protect the psyche from what it can't bear to contemplate steadily. The threat of naked vision is a fearful one.

For a man on the rack, or in the act of drowning, there is no language that is not a mockery. Something like that perspective is intimated by the pokerfaced mouthers of stereotypes who inhabit the theater of the absurd—Ionescans, for example, who talk to keep from seeing how weird they are and how fragile their existence is. So is it, on some level, for all of us. In the classic experiment, a man with nothing to see, hear, or feel—in the closest possible approximation to zero sensation—calls on his own voice to bear him company. As long as he can keep that monologue going, he's keeping catatonia at bay. It's like an emblem of the last game, which only the multiplicity of our blessed enemies in the here and now keeps us from having to play.

If I don't kill that rat, he'll die.
BECKETT, *Endgame*

Invective and Insult

Standing under the dust clouds on the plains of windy Troy, the heroes exchange boasts and insults before they come to blows. Neither insults nor boasts are very elaborate, for the situation hardly allows of elaboration. The strongest word of insult is normally "Dog," embellished occasionally with a bit of grim humor or derision; the biggest brags are genealogical, when a man points to his deep-rooted, many-branched family tree, and dares his foe to stand up against *that*. After spear and sword have done their gruesome work, the victor often exults over his fallen enemy, sometimes imagining how news of the man's death will be received at home, sometimes describing in detail who the victim was and where he came from: "Trojans, tell haughty Iloneus' beloved father / and mother, from me, that they can weep for him in their halls, since / neither shall the wife of Promachos,

Alegenor's / son, take pride of delight in her dear lord's coming, on that day / when we sons of the Achaians come home from Troy in our vessels." Or again, "Lie there, Otrynteus' son, most terrifying of all men. / Here is your death, but your generation was by the lake waters / of Gyge, where is the allotted land of your fathers / by fish-swarming Hyllos, and the whirling waters of Hermos" (*Iliad,* 14,500 and 20,389, tr. Lattimore).

Clearly the boast before battle serves to give the warrior a full grasp on his own individuality, to nerve him for the encounter; under those circumstances, he will give his enemy credit for as little courage and dignity as necessary, he is a "Dog." But when the foe lies dead, the gloat requires one to say as amply as possible who he was, even to give him credit for nobility of spirit and lofty lineage. For of course he is no longer a threat to one's ego, but an enhancement of it.

Much of the warfare in the *Iliad* is brutal and anonymous: in one terrible auditory image, Homer compares the sound of battle to the swift, thudding strokes of a company of woodmen dismembering a tree with their axes. But whenever individual heroes meet in a clear space, the rapid counterpoint of boasting, insulting, killing, and exulting makes much of the texture of the poem; and insult runs through all three of the verbal ingredients that surround the act of murder—self-glory reflects discredit if not shame on the enemy, posthumous praise of him reflects still more glory on his killer. For a good part of this performance, the enemy is not much more than a pretext. Insult is of course a contrast of ego with ego, but it is also a contrast of ego with alien violence—a defiance shouted at the world and its ultimate power, of which the immediate antagonist is no more than a passing representative. And this character insult may still share, though surrounded by a whole repertoire of playful and mocking gestures, from which it is distinguished, sometimes, only by a fleeting facial expression: "When you call me that, podnuh, *smile!*"

It is in the highest degree curious that modern society has developed so few formal ways of distinguishing between friendly banter and deadly insult. For most of our edged weapons the mores have provided a sheath; only the most primitive safeguards protect us from giving or receiving insult. Particularly is this true of our pluralistic, cosmopolitan society, where the patron of a nightclub may be savagely abused without provocation, think himself highly entertained, tip his tormentor generously—yet then step tipsily into the street, make a wrong gesture or misspeak himself with blurry jocosity, and wind up the evening on a marble slab, from sheer clumsiness in manipulating the terminology and implications of insult.

The range here is wider than we commonly realize. When men fought duels as a matter of course, insult could be and often was an elegantly minimal affair. To tap a man on the shoulder and nod curtly at him was to set in motion the machinery of seconds, weapons, time, place, and ultimately, no doubt, the services of

doctor, priest, and undertaker. Whether the challenger
was really insulted or not, the man challenged certainly
was—the first and second causes of dispute, however
intricate their essential differences, giving rise to the
same inexorable process. The word "lie," however
circumspectly pronounced (though to be sure in those
distant days nobody had yet thought of the exquisite
euphemism, "credibility gap"), led with similar directness to swords or pistols. That was the rule among
gentlemen, of course; another rule prevailed among
jarveys and fishwives, or on the stage, where the
playwright's motives (professional and personal alike)
might easily get entwined with those of his characters.
Between superficial jest and terrible deep earnest,
characters in Shakespeare frequently abuse one
another as vociferously, as grossly, and as inventively
as any student of dysphuism could want. When Kent
berates Cornwall's steward, for example, it is partly
because he wants to provoke a fight with a man he
despises, but also because his (and perhaps Shakespeare's) rage with this gross pragmatical pig of a
world o'erflows all measure—he must unpack his
heart with words, and so he does:

Steward: What dost thou know me for?
Kent: A knave, a rascal, an eater of broken meats; a base,
proud, shallow, beggarly, three-suited, hundred-pound,
filthy, worsted-stocking knave; a lily-livered, action-taking
knave; a whoreson, glass-gazing, super-serviceable finical
rogue; a one-trunk inheriting slave; one that wouldst be a
bawd in way of good service, and art nothing but the composition of a knave, beggar, coward, pandar, and the son

and heir of a mongrel bitch; one whom I will beat into clamorous whining if thou deniest the least syllable of thy addition.

It is evidently the "nothing" quality of the steward, his utter pliability and servility, that so infuriate Kent at this point; his insults are a defiance of the cosmos, whose indifference enrages him more than would its active personal hostility. Outrageous insult is here in effect an explosion in behalf of one's exasperated humanity.

One broaches no great novelty in proposing that insult is surrogate aggression, or that aggression embodies, as often as not, hostility to more than its immediate target, and likely more than hostility itself. But the total unpredictability of contemporary responses to insult or supposed insult—given the fact that insult is itself a tangled and deeply rooted emotional act—is something new. Perhaps the popularity of the stand-up and put-down comedian is due to his appealing combination of safety and danger. He offers conflict, but one in which he, if anybody, is going to get punched in the nose—and the chances of its going that far are pretty slim. Trading insults with him massages the customer's ego (he has, after all, stood up to a professional), and relieves his tensions (there's a man in the home office to whom he's always wanted to say just that). If only symbolically, the conflict has been real, though also pseudo; "real" is used here in the sense of "personal," not wholly surrogate or paper-doll. In a world where so much is prearranged and predictable, the customer has taken a very small chance, and feels more of a man afterwards. Insults given and taken have acted as abrasive stimulants to his latent virility, as they were for the Homeric heroes.

Deep insult has, naturally, been avoided with care. Even in a pretty rough nightclub, you cannot call a man "the son and heir of a mongrel bitch," and expect him to be amused by your wit. In addition, racial slurs and epithets are completely out—not because they aren't present in men's minds, but because they very much are, along with a set of possible reactions to them, so if they were used, "the whole situation would get out of hand." In a word, they are too dangerous, they touch levels that are too explosive to be publicly handled. In another direction, and for other reasons, there are off-limit subjects of insult (physical handicaps and deformities, for instance, or aspects of a woman's person) which will quickly forfeit audience sympathy. Out of the overall requirement that he be entertaining, the comedian draws still other, less distinctly formulated taboos and compulsions: he cannot dwell on a topic, but must keep moving; he must take a joke better than he gives one, and carefully cultivate the most cutting of his antagonists—he cannot lose anything important through his opponent's being witty, since the audience simply gets two comedians for the price of one.

In real life, where an ill-timed insult can get you hit and hurt and maybe even badly hurt, the rules of the game are far harder to define. The traditional deep insults are fecal, sexual, and familial; but they vary widely in energy and relevance from culture to culture, and in a mixed culture it's particularly hard to tell how much vitality they retain. An observer from another time or climate might well find it both evident and odd that Anglo-Saxons have almost no way of abusing a man with the implication that he's a cuckold. The very word has an artificial, antiquarian tone about it, as of bodkins and codpieces. Whereas, in Italy, a very casual and indeed accidental gesture, suggesting but only remotely horns, has been known to earn an unfortunate innocent six inches of stiletto under the ribs. (An entire area around Seminara in Calabria has recently undergone devastation because of a vendetta arising from one such gesture.) Writing some years ago, Robert Graves reported from Arabic countries a usage even more alien to our mores: the ultimate insult, the last word spoken before knives and broken bottles were invoked, was customarily "brother-in-law." It was a potent term because it implied that the insultor had enjoyed the favors of the insultee's sister—hence that the brother was incapable of protecting or avenging the family honor. But how could either of these insults long retain their virulence in an age of diffused and diverse and often fractured families, not to speak of women's liberation? They imply a degree of personal responsibility on the part of man for woman, and a sense that female promiscuity is ultimately shameful, that people simply don't share any more.

The terminology is largely obsolete, yet for purposes of deep insult, these sexual expressions are almost the only ones we've got. Surely the most-used words of insult in contemporary America are "bastard" and "son of a bitch," neither of which is more than remotely symbolic in its application. When we refer to a politician as either or both, we mean nothing more than that he is effective and unscrupulous. The addition of a single neutral adjective will come close to turning either term into a tribute. A "clever bastard," or a "tough son of a bitch" are phrases of half-affectionate admiration from an impressed opponent. The abusive use of both expressions is no doubt a hold-over from the day when bastards were seriously thought to be more disagreeable and contemptible than legitimate scions. But of course what the terms really impugn, rather than the individual, is his mother, who has nothing to do with the case. Insulting her is therefore gratuitous, therefore a deliberate *casus belli*—the insulter is signalling his readiness for conflict. In their literal sense, most such signal-terms are irrelevant and absurd; but under the conditions of insult, they are read with an eye to their intent, not their meaning, and so convey their message with perfect clarity.

The "conditions of insult" are more numerous and particular than one might think offhand. For example, insult is always a face-to-face affair. You can slander a man in the public prints (and for that his recourse is the law), but you cannot insult him. Further, persistence is a great point of insult. The insulter must be advised, unless it's completely obvious that he knows already, that what he says is offensive; if he then persists, the insult is "serious." It's no accident that the phrase, "Say that again," plays so large a part in the forming-up of quarrels, for it's an act of verification by which one looks behind words at personal intents. Without personal intent on both sides, there can hardly be insult. It is difficult indeed to insult, though you may despise or ridicule, a collectivity, a corporation, or a legislative body. You cannot readily insult a man who assumes his innate and therefore artificial superiority to you; for insult is an inherently democratic form of address, implying a relation, as we say, of "man to man." To challenge a gentleman, you have to be a gentleman yourself; you can't disdain a man whom both of you recognize as a social superior, and he can't disdain you without rubbing in his advantage unworthily. Being out of the ordinary range, presidents are as hard to insult as priests or pariahs; and kings, it's to be suspected, can be insulted only by other kings.

Any scheme for distinguishing modes and styles of insult opens an almost limitless field of particularities. The really elaborate insult has to be playful in some degree if it's not to perish under its own weight. Ingenious conflicts of light insult have often served as parlor games, as between Beatrice and Benedick in *Much Ado,* or in the rougher medieval "flyting" of the Scottish poets Dunbar and Kennedy. Like stage duellists or antagonists in an opera vowing eternal hatred in an intricately woven duet, insult-contestants generally keep an eye cocked on the audience. But when Milton abuses Salmasius like a fishwife with an unexpectedly copious Latin vocabulary, he is far too solemn in his vituperation for the comfort of the reader. There is even something oppressive in the rigor with which Dryden and Pope go about savaging an opponent:

> Spiteful he is not, though he wrote a satire,
> For still there goes some thinking to ill nature:
> He needs no more than birds or beasts to think,
> All his occasions are to eat and drink.
> If he call rogue and rascal from a garret,
> He means you no more mischief than a parrot;
> The words for friend and foe alike were made,
> To fetter 'em in verse is all his trade,
> For almonds he'll cry whore to his own mother,
>
> > etc., etc.

Except for trying to be mean, the passage itself sounds as careless of what it is saying as the man it describes; it rattles along with a kind of slatternly, scolding energy that is perhaps its chief attractiveness, but that also starts quickly to sound like an empty tin can. There may be some exquisite humor in the satirist sounding exactly like the man he's satirizing, but it's not pointed or clear enough to avoid battering the ear and deadening the mind.

Even though it can't really avoid a tendency toward verbal oversupply, the invective mode needn't fall victim to it, for self-mockery deftly converts a failing to a point of strength. When Rabelais is describing how

the cake-bakers of Lerné responded to a modest request by their neighbors the grape-growers, nothing
is clearer than that he, and his translators Urquhart and
Motteux took the occasion as a pretext for virtuoso
vocabulary-display. The cake-bakers not only de-
clined to sell the grape-growers cakes at the regular
market rate:

> but (which was worse) did injure them most outra-
> geously, calling them prattling gabblers, licorous gluttons,
> freckled bittors, mangy rascals, shite-a-bed scoundrels,
> drunken roysterers, sly knaves, drowsy loiterers, slapsauce
> fellows, slubberdegullion druggles, lubbardly louts, cozen-
> ing foxes, ruffian rogues, paultry customers, sycophant-
> varlets, drawlatch hoydens, flouting milksops, jeering com-
> panions, staring clowns, forlorn snakes, ninny lobcocks,
> scurvy sneaksbies, fondling fops, base loons, saucy cox-
> combs, idle lusks, scoffing braggards, noddy meacocks,
> blockish grutnols, doddi-pol jolt-heads, jobbernol goose-
> caps, foolish loggerheads, flutch calf-lollies, grouthead
> gnat-snappers, lob-dotterels, gaping changelings, codshead
> loobies, woodcock slangams, ninnie-hammer fly-catchers,
> noddiepeak simpletons, turdy-gut shitten shepherds, and
> other such like defamatory epithets.

It's very hard to improve on this as an instance of the
insult vociferous; and one notes especially the way it
draws attention from the insultee to the insultor, balanced as he is precariously on his commitment to an
unbroken stream of invention. He cannot repeat, he
cannot hesitate, he cannot descend from the whirlwind
of his language even to consider the occasion of it.

Ornate and vociferous insults may thus extend themselves magnificently, but at the expense of depth and dignity; the rush of particulars gives no time for implications to sink in, and the prominence of the insultor, as a mannered or even ridiculous speaker, slips him toward easy identification with the insultee. The Insult Majestic, or baroque insult, may or may not involve subtleties, but its weight and dignity set the speaker immediately on a plane wholly different from his victim's. Legend has it, for example, that Professor Mahaffy was once chatting with a colleague in a corridor of Trinity College when a desperate student interrupted him to ask where was the men's room. "At the end of this corridor," said majestic Mahaffy, pointing, "you will find a door marked GENTLEMEN: but don't let that stop you." Such a put-down is rather broad and explicit than otherwise; but the insult majestic may embody considerable duplicity of thought and even a delayed explosion of implication. Doctor Johnson, being rowed down the Thames by a sculler, was assailed from the shore (as custom then was) by a foulmouthed fellow with a very generous flow of invective. Having endured as much as a man decently could, he turned on the scurrilist and said loudly and deliberately, "Sir, your mother, under pretext of keeping a bawdy house, was a receiver of stolen goods." The subordinate clause provides at once the balance and the dynamic of this insult. "Under pretext of" gives evidence of judicious discrimination between appearance and reality; yet it implies that the man's mother, casting about for the most decent front she could find for her fencing operations, could imagine nothing better than running a bawdy house. There is no way to make pretext or pretense of running a bawdy house except by running one, so that implication stands too. It is an extraordinarily opulent sentence; yet balanced, objective, and perfectly simple. One would like to think the recipient took it home and thought about it for several weeks.

In much the same vein is a pronunciamento of Bill Klem, the Old Arbitrator, to a quarrelsome batter who was protesting a called third strike. "Sir, you are an applehead!" Here no latent subtleties cry out for exegesis, no hazy definition requires resolution. It is one of those heavy pronouncements to which the English declarative sentence lends itself. Not an implication or an overtone impairs the dignity of the speaker; his key word falls with the impact of a cleaver, but it is not, and was not, a cliché. "Applehead" has the special aroma of a word invented or discovered perhaps in a rural setting, ripened in the speaker's mind for years, and exploded at this moment against the one tedious numskull in the major leagues fatuous enough to deserve it.

The pace of modern life has quickened, of course, and the range of modern expression has broadened; simple slogan-insults, like "capitalist running dogs," "imperialist lackeys," or "male chauvinist pigs" seem therefore particularly inappropriate, explicable only through an absolute lack of verbal imagination.

Brighter, sharper, quicker as a retort to surliness and truculence are the metallic smile, the flashing thumb, and the murmured phrase, "Up yours." C. S. Lewis once answered a polite and lucrative invitation to lecture in America with a surly negative hand-written on toilet paper; that is curmudgeonly behavior of the old school, which isolates the insulter in his private rage, instead of making him free of the civilized world. It merited, if such were possible, the trans-Atlantic thumb.

A proper insulter rises above his own insult; it should be grossly rude, foul if possible, but happy in its delivery. Neither the provocation nor the rebuke will touch the skilled insulter, isolated in his gaiety. I am not sure if Dorothy Parker should be given credit for the classic repartee, involving a young actress who stood aside to let her pass through a doorway, muttering, "Age before beauty." Miss Parker swept through, tossing over her shoulder the perfect non-parallel, "And pearls before swine." Crisp, ringing, and terminal, this phrase is a paragon of the modern throwaway insult.

Below or alongside the insult direct (which, as we've implied, is a noble and therefore an increasingly peripheral art form) exist all sorts of slights and put-downs which rankle like insult but ought to be distinguished from it. Odious familiarity, for example is a form of implicit insult, a gross instance of which is mechanized personal communication. A hearty, hand-written, nostalgic, mimeographed document arrives, signed by someone you never heard of, inviting you to a class reunion, and misspelling your name. An unctuous politician or an oily moralist includes you among a group of people with whom you wouldn't be caught dead; a salesman or manipulator tries to worm his way into your confidence with a "personalized" line and an obviously specious intent. Particularly hateful is the experience of being included in a group of right-minded citizens whom in fact one considers sanctimonious bigots; but handlers and touchers (who at first acquaintance pat you on the back or wrap a good-fellow arm around your shoulders) are also obnoxious. The story may not be true, but it is characteristic of both men, that effusive Hubert Humphrey (when he was a Presidential candidate) once bustled up to Frank Sinatra (when he was a Democrat) and tugged the sleeve of his jacket. "Hands off the threads, creep," was the response he got; and, though it hurts to say so, just this once the thin man was right.

Indignities of this nature are exasperating, to be sure, but only in extreme cases do they reach a grossness which amounts to positive insult; and even then, it's as much a matter of circumstances as of the act itself. One moment of classic, almost poetic, disgust occurs in *Lolita,* when Humbert's first wife has decided to leave him for a White Russian taxi-driver. The three sit for a while in the Humbert living room, discussing this turn of events; the "lover" excuses himself to go to the john, and after the two of them have left together, Humbert, inspecting the bathroom, finds that the toilet has not been flushed, and a dead cigarette butt is floating in the pool of urine.

As a discarded husband floating in a pool of self-disgust, Humbert is of course particularly sensitive to that language of gesture which is a frequent dialect of discourtesy and boorishness. In other circumstances, he might feel revulsion or contempt, but not murder-ous hatred. Indeed, abominable rudeness is so much the rule in the affairs of this world that only a thick skin and an indifferent disposition keep us from bleeding to death most of the days of our life. Who doesn't know the wandering eye and vacant expression of the "friend" who isn't really interested in our grievance or our project, even though he pretended to be? The pseudo-listener and his counterpart the monopolistic nothing-sayer, those established short circuits of meaningful conversation, put us down more brutally, sometimes, than if they looked straight at us, and spat in our eye. Yet their "nothing" behavior passes in most circles as a sort of manners, and there's no need to expand the word "insult" to cover it.

Below rudeness and coldness and the half-insult of deliberate indifference lies a still more delicate flower, more difficult to discriminate and describe, which we can call the buried insult, or insult reflexive. It gener-ally rises from the implied perception that the insulter is so far superior to the insulted that he must make enormous efforts to prevent that obvious fact from becoming socially painful. Yet he can't be associated with the folly of the insultee; he must set himself apart.

This he does by yielding to the victim's aims and intents, endorsing them, approving them, and yet pushing them ever so slightly toward the ludicrous. Where the victim is already pushing a little too hard, one overcomplies, and pulls him, off-balance, into the faintly absurd—a fate from which one may or may not rescue him. An allied device (used, for example, when an outsider is introduced into a group of insiders) is an excess of politeness, such a profusion of polite forms and formulas, that their purpose becomes plain—that is, the prevention of any other form of converse. The first of these devices is known, in traditional terminology, as "humoring a fool to the top of his bent," except that in the situation as given it's not altogether clear who's the fool. The second has no name, but is exactly described by Stendhal in accounting for Julien Sorel's position in Hôtel de la Mole: during the entire day, says the novelist, his self-esteem was never wounded, yet at the end of it he was ready to weep. It is a curious and special use of the vapid (perhaps a natural vapidity) for purposes of humiliation.

Stupidity used to be the ground-bass of insult; the Book of Proverbs devotes itself rather liberally to insulting the "fool" and defining the various forms of his foolishness. All such talk about foolishness and fools who partake of it naturally implies an assurance that an established wisdom exists, ready to hand and comprehensible by the docile though untrained mind, of which a man cannot fail unless he is much to blame. To say the least, that view is much less defensible now than it used to be. In addition, the whole notion of "wisdom" is a lot more dubious than formerly, since the individual has so much less command of his own destiny, and his own qualities count for less. In a tribal society, wisdom and experience yield a man authority; in a democratic megalopolis, they qualify him for social security and medicare. Stupidity has even taken on special positive values in our day: apart from its value as a preliminary stage of what is often called "sincerity," there are jargons in which it is "elitist" to be anything but stupid, and ways of life within which the prime end is stupefaction. Apart from these self-enclosed enclaves, there are circumstances in which being wise really does seem like a roundabout and pretentious way of being stupid. Now that "culture" is no longer an unquestioned value, but "nature" has its vociferous claims to counterpose, the sacred fool (who has always been reverenced) may turn out to be merely the natural one. Finally, words like "cretin," "moron," and "idiot" have taken on new colorings as a result of a new humane attitude toward mental disease. They make us think of misfortune and misery, rather than complacent foolishness. Here, as with sexist jokes and insults, or racial stereotypes, we come up against the fact that "controversial" really is a disqualifying word, all by itself. This is simply because, amid explanations and qualifications and retractions, the joke and insult alike wilt and wither and lose point. Both the absurd and the outrageous imply something like an absolute, or at least a generally accepted, standard of what is neither. As a pluralistic society can only count on the very broadest parodies of human behavior seeming generally funny, so it must limit its insults to those few blunt, familiar weapons which don't automatically rebound against the wielder, or turn in his hand. In the specific instance, holding mere stupidity against a man is certainly undemocratic and probably un-American as well.

Indeed, the more arguable and indefinite the conditions of insult become, the more the moral burden of insult existing at all falls on the victim. If he weren't abnormally sensitive—the straightforward word is "paranoid"—he wouldn't see insult where somebody else (who pretends to be "normal" but merely has variant hangups) doesn't. The whole idea that there's a statistical norm for insult, to which a man can be held whether or not he's given consent, or even heard of it, is itself insulting. If A isn't entitled to feel insulted where B wouldn't, then B isn't entitled to feel insult where C wouldn't, and so on to the end of the alphabet and around again, in pursuit of someone who has less self-respect than anyone else. Perhaps such a lowest common denominator can ultimately be found; taking him as a norm seems like opting for sheepish and supine insensitivity as a social value in itself.

We revolt, then; we are revolted at the process of a world socially lobotomized into tranquility; we declare our personal standards of what is and what is not insulting. And at once the world turns into a nightmare of traps and windstorms. In the matter of insult, both given and taken, I look on myself (who am no more than typical) as an absolute impenetrable maze. How can any decent trial-and-error American citizen, of the sort I live among, possibly anticipate the things that cause me to blow up—when half the time they take even me, who have been trying to get used to them for fifty years, completely by surprise? I have a foul temper and a placatory disposition. Snobs, anti-semites, cliques, and public liars anger me consistently—that's very noble, I daresay; but so do the rude, even those whom others call, not without admiration, "frank." I am, I think, a violent, narrow man, and very apt to be cruel with those who offend my standard of manners, also with a lot of people who differ from me in style and simply in opinion. Yet, knowing all this about myself, and disliking most of it, I am still more intolerant of contempt, and equally of obsequiousness, than anyone else I know. Probably this is only because I know myself in ways that I don't know other people. But how is a stranger to guess anything like this about me? My intolerance of the rude goes along with an active liking for the independent-minded. How do I discriminate these two categories? I really don't know; and if I don't know, how can I expect others to deal with me as I expect them to? The situation may be less unfair than it seems because most people have options and alterna-tives before they have to commit themselves to very much coping with me. But that particular reflection doesn't mitigate very much. As a class, I tend to like people with abrasive tongues; but when they're used on me, not just in fun, but with real sincerity (I sometimes have to guess between these alternatives, but not real hard), I guess I don't like it any better than anybody else. With two hundred million people in this country, each of them similarly compounded of boobytraps, bristling with hostilities, and quivering with resentments, it's a marvel that we're not all at each other's throats.

One basic fact about insult is that we're all afraid of it; for it can be an unpredictably abrupt short-cut out of the sphere of language altogether. A gang of wild chimpanzees, confronted with a stuffed leopard, use the chimpanzee equivalent of insult as a danger-measuring device. From the safety of trees, they yammer and yack at the enemy, they hurl bits of stick and trash at him. Growing bolder, they dash at him, shouting fiercely, and then scamper quickly away. Our laughter at their behavior is tinged with complacency because we know from the beginning that the leopard is stuffed. But they have never seen a stuffed leopard in their lives, and have no way of imagining that such a thing exists. We in our civilized world do not encounter many live leopards—they are rather a sharp surprise when they turn on us, with operational teeth and claws, after approaching under cover of a gray flannel suit, or in the unlikely veldt of an academic library. I'm not one of them myself, having a little streak of chimpanzee as uneasy neighbor to what there is of leopard in me. But I've seen and felt enough of the duplicities to sense that insult is a good place to apply Blake's hellish proverb: "One law for the lion and the ox is tyranny." It works equally well with leopards and chimpanzees. Perhaps this is a special reason for accepting confusion as the best of all possible conditions surrounding insult; it may well be too dangerous and too intimate a practice to be trusted to the adjudication of the merely rational mind.

Men have been killed with leather swords, and insult and invective, even after we've surrounded them with all the cotton wool at our disposal, are still felt to provide the potential for dangerous fun. I think they are used now, more to prevent our getting into serious conflict, than to provoke it, but they wouldn't serve their full role in the economy of the malicious man, if they didn't do both at once. With a minimum of management, they enable him to feel like a deadly leopard while remaining a chattering chimpanzee. Society at the moment seems to ask nothing better.

En allemand c'est mentir que d'être poli.
GOETHE

The New Arts of Political Lying

Since this subject was first broached about 1710 (in two anonymous folio volumes which survive, alas, only in a popular summary of the first), the arts of political lying have undergone the sort of explosive change and development that we associate with modern technology. Earlier students of the subject had, no doubt, their very legitimate insights, and for their day, we may concede that they developed the topic acceptably. But that was more than two and a half centuries ago; the naiveté of that remote age is suggested by the effort of the authors actually to cover their chosen field in two volumes. Twenty *Encyclopedia Britannica's* would not suffice, nowadays, for a prolegomenon to a systematic treatise of political lying; and the present wispy sketch (written with the brevity of desperation) aims only to be the precursor of a proper foreword—a mere golliwog of the cosmos microprinted on the head of a pin. For political lying has entered, in our day, the era of mass production. A standardized and uniform article is concocted by disciplined teams of workmen, each operator exercising only a single primitive skill, performing only a minute part of the total operation, and bearing no real responsibility for the final artifact. Millions of units can thus be manufactured at a very cheap price indeed; and if their life expectancy is short, so much the better. Instant obsolescence is one of the chief beauties of the new political lie.

That antique discussion of 1710 strikes us as strange mainly because it takes for granted that a man who creates political lies does so of set purpose, shaping and adjusting them like a craftsman to the ends for which they were designed. That was doubtless normal practice in the age of handicraft, when a man made artifacts to last his own time, if not longer. But nowadays political lying is as natural as breathing used to be, and the lie need last no longer than from one breath to the next. The individual lie is nothing, the structure of collective lying is as inclusive as, and not much less tightly knit than, the medieval church. The only act for which deliberate individual calculation is required is an occasional effort to speak political truth. Perhaps a partial exception should be made here for the genuine virtuoso in the art of mendacity. When he gets very good indeed, we are likely to dismiss his performance, not without contempt, as mere "second nature." But this judgment is certainly too facile. There may well be principles of art in the high political lie, which analysis would reveal—especially in the techniques of compulsory lying, or lying under pressure, where a man's free flow of native fancy is inhibited.

But if we are ever to contemplate nuances of this sort, we must disqualify at once the lie drab and routine, the dogmatic, exclusive ideological lie which prevails in full hideousness through wide areas of the world we inhabit. This is not strictly political lying, for under a totalitarian regime in the modern style, what little dissent there is can express itself only as intrigue—where, indeed, the classic arts of conspiracy, calumny, and double-cross find free play. But outside the ruling clique, politics as the art of persuasion and deception hardly exists. What the state says at the moment is automatically right; he who disagrees is by definition either a criminal or a madman, and his natural destination is either a labor camp or a *maison de force.* Should the unhappy dissident try to be informed from any source other than the official, he is impeded by every means at the disposal of the authorities. His mail is opened, his telephone is bugged, he is refused access to foreign newspapers or magazines, foreign radio programs are kept from his ears by jamming, foreign visitors are kept from talking to him by policemen. Should he try to escape physically, his way is barred by a wall, manned by guards who shoot to kill. Access to the very past is destroyed by the systematic updating of encyclopedias and works of reference; art, literature, and music are monitored to ensure conformity with the current party line. All these events are so commonplace, one is ashamed to recite them; and of course the system involves massive lying as a matter of routine, the active perpetration of innumerable falsehoods, the silent suppression of innumerable truths. But it is lying on such a grandiose scale, so shameless and blatant in the face of the sun, as scarcely to be lying at all. Whatever else can be said of him, a robber who approaches his victim in broad daylight with an axe in one hand and a pistol in the other, cannot properly be accused of fraud. When powerful nations approach variant versions of truth with blackjack and straightjacket, we may mourn, as at a frightful wound to the mind; but we had best turn here to crimes of a more human dimension and disposition.

All skating on thin ice is properly divided into free-form and fixed-routine exercises, since the two disciplines clearly demand distinct talents. Free-form lying shades at its upper reach into mere temperamental enthusiasm, verbal embroidery, or that natural deficiency of critical energy in the prefrontal lobes which is characteristic of salesmen. Any candidate for dogcatcher in any hayseed county of this nation would be thought half-hearted and bashful in his quest for office if he didn't assert loudly that his election would be followed by instant millennium. This is the kind of exaggeration that the Roman law condoned under the heading of *"dolus bonus,"* a proper fraud, such as overcomes any enthusiastic advocate for a cause or product. It is not a perversion of human nature, but human nature itself; we all make allowances for it. No man of normal common sense believes every word spoken to him by a used-car salesman wearing a red tie and a funny hat. Neither does he accuse the rogue of lying if the $225 creampuff turns out after experience to have a fault here and a flaw there—to consist, in fact, mostly of faults and flaws. The salesman was just hopeful. That's what he's paid for. When interest is involved, most men exaggerate, and the more freely when dealing with intangibles, where practical tests don't apply, and even distinct syntax isn't often expected.

Indistinctness is the essence of free-form lying in its higher manifestations, of which politics is just one. The artist in this medium blurs, confuses, and deliberately talks in such abstractions as will invite every reader to project into them his own particulars. He need say very little as long as he implies a lot. Indeed, mere association often works more potently than coherent assertion, as ads which portray sexy girls with cars don't actually promise that you'll get the girl if you get the car (and wouldn't carry conviction if they did), but intimate it nonetheless. Subliminal suggestion of this sort, which lies under the threshold of consciousness, is often circumangular as well—it hints of what lies around the corner from direct vision and is therefore all the more intriguing. The higher modes of political lying make use of the same enthymeme, working it negatively as well as positively. By supporting Candidate A, the voter will indeed be aligning himself with Shirley MacLaine, Abraham

Lincoln, Pericles, Lenny Bernstein, and Saint Paul; he is also opposing, in Rascal B, Jack the Ripper, Jefferson Davis, George the Third, and all the historic evil a single citizen can incorporate. Though the details of a sweeping political contrast can safely be left unexpressed, they can also be spread across ill-defined straw-men and mythical figureheads, whose black-hearted designs and fatuous opinions can be contrasted to advantage with the golden integrity of Our Hero. Any field of magnetic force is useful in politics; and a good strong negative is often so valuable as to become, in itself, positive. Radicals and reactionaries, because they use one another so freely in their propaganda, are often observed to develop a symbiotic relationship. They study one another's rhetoric, polemicize against one another's outrageous behavior, inflate one another as bogeymen for scaring timid neutrals in a desired direction. In short, they depend on one another so largely that their verbal opposition, even when rhetorically sincere, may become manipulatively a political lie. The counterpart of the kiss of death is the war of convenience; the aims of radical students often dovetail beautifully with those of reactionary politicians, and a stream of further particulars suggest themselves.

"Tying things together" is a device of political lying, or at least extrapolation, particularly frequent and handy for developing a paranoid view of history. Nothing hostile to one's chosen interests is presumed to happen independently of a vast structure of plotting in which the most remote and dissimilar elements are secretly engaged. Revolutionary and counter-revolutionary customarily agree on the definition of this warfare, except that each attributes the vast scheme exclusively to the other side. Whatever serves our *parti pris* is a spontaneous act of idealism; whatever the antagonist does is the act of robots being manipulated by a crafty central agency of master-plotters. What this suggests is that guilt-by-association is stronger in a propaganda sense than glory-by-association. And it is mainly in this respect, by changing positive for negative association-patterns, that modern ingenuity has been able to add appreciably to the achievement of earlier ages. Nineteenth-century tear-jerkers like Daniel Webster, William Jennings Bryan, and their ilk, stand beyond or apart from contemporary practice. Their windbaggery tended to associate them or their causes with a visionary company of heroic idealists. Modern style aims to associate the enemy (through evidence if possible, despite it if necessary) with an alien and oppressive force. They are the weavers of evil, mysterious and deadly agents of global politics, while the forces of good are all spontaneous, individual, and therefore conveniently vague.

A little below this sort of high-flying lie, whether manic or paranoid, we enter upon the vast kingdom of the ideological lie proper, so much of which we have already placed outside this discussion. Hateful as it is in its frozen, official form, the ideological lie in its early stages may be simply lying in the optative mood—

hopeful, even creative lying. One has a project in mind, the unification, say, of a group of radically disparate citizens into a cohesive group, large enough to elect one to a desirable public office. The first, negative step is to avoid all reference to divisive differences; they exist, of course, they are on everyone's mind, but there is obviously nothing to be done about them. Then one exaggerates such bonds of unity as can be found or imagined, not because they are inherently strong or important, but in the hope of making them a bit stronger and more important than they are. Technically, this is *suppressio veri* in the first instance and *commissio falsi* in the second; but the persuasive situation, the obvious and avowed advocacy of the speaker, are powerful mitigants. Human behavior being as unpredictable as it is, there has to be room in politics for trial and error; and here, even though a man may be thoroughly mistaken, he is only by indirect construction and remote implication a political liar. But from this tentative and experimental testing of the political waters, it is only a short step to that kind of categorical rigidity which sees the world as an abstract scheme, and chops particular observations long or short to fit (Procrustes-like) that scheme.

Forgetting inconvenient complexities is very easy and natural when one is absorbed in a struggle. Most advocates of good causes—the opponents of war, liquor, drugs, poverty, prejudice, inequality, oppression, pollution—fail to consider the second problem, that of finding a moral or social equivalent for the

particular horror they are eager to abolish. I'm not
implying that all the particular abuses listed above are
equivalent, or that it isn't sometimes necessary to
abolish a flagrant and crying abuse before one knows
what exact institution will replace it. One-sided or partial or imperfectly worked-out views of a topic don't
necessarily involve political lying; but when obtuseness becomes so deliberate and systematic that it
amounts to refusal to face the facts (they are "stubborn
things" as Lenin said), political lying is not very far
away. The first victim of the political liar in such circumstances is very often himself; and he is encouraged
in his elected form of political myopia by the current
custom of dividing an intricate social complex into a
number of so-called "problems," as if those problems
could always be solved one at a time and in isolation
from one another. We will solve the poverty problem
when nobody is poor any more; as for the problems
that this "solution" will create, we will think of them
when the time comes. This procedure of consciously
closing one's eyes to the consequences of a policy one
has decided to advocate may be placed in a separate
subdivision as a methodological lie. There is, or may
still be, something forgivably human about this deliberate specializing of one's concern, one's focusing on a
single area of existence. The English middle classes
(perhaps as one more hangover from their empire) are
famous for a passionate involvement with neglected or
suffering animals which it is facile to contrast with
their indifference to the fate of neglected or suffering

people. Of course we cannot all be aware at every moment of all the wrongs in the world; even if there is a man in Senegal who may be hungrier and is doubtless more deserving than the cat on my doorstep, it is a lie for me to use the one as an excuse for refusing the other—since I have no serious intention of doing something significant in Senegal, and if I don't aid the cat, she will surely die.

Yet closing one's eyes is the chief characteristic of the inhuman ideological lie; it proceeds on its relentless way under the slogan, "I don't know, I don't want to know, don't try to tell me." When Señor Castro declares, with a straight face and in the presence of witnesses, that the Soviet Union is the disinterested and idealistic servant of humanity, it is because he has hypnotized himself with ideology. If one asked him about the suppression of various national movements, of which Hungary and Czechoslovakia can stand for many, presumably he would say the people who led those movements were not spokesmen for humanity, were not, in fact, human. He does not know what they feel and does not want to know. Perhaps the most disturbing thing about this sort of ideological lie is the liar's assurance that "his side" will survive to write the textbooks, and can therefore be counted on to represent a lie with the right bias as ultimate truth. Ideology of this sort can lead a man to deny the direct evidence of his senses. Some years ago, I read in a copy of *Le Monde* (a French journal with some reputation for accuracy) an account of the way in which black students were systematically excluded from the City College of New York, while white students were bussed cross-town through Harlem to go there. The statement would be more ludicrous now than it was then; but there has been no time in the last forty years when it was not false in its entirety. The story was date-lined New York: the reporter pretended to be an eyewitness of the events he described. But his ideological blinkers told him the United States was a racist, discriminatory society (an assumption which, as qualified, might even be true in certain senses), and so caused him to invent, crudely and clumsily enough, a morality-scene that he could not possibly have witnessed.

At the very root of the ideological lie, smaller in scale, more pervasive and perhaps more insidious, but leading into the blacker evil, is something which can be called the systematic or schematic lie. Institutions are set up to operate in certain ways; people enter them, and they no longer operate as they were "supposed" to. The real channels in any organization follow different lines than are shown on the organization chart. Miss Whipplethorpe, Vice-President Eggplant's secretary, is the mainspring of the operation—her boss is a numskull. Everyone knows that the way to get things done is to talk to Miss Whipplethorpe and avoid Eggplant—yet the organizational forms have to be respected, and Eggplant finds himself signing documents and getting credit for ideas of which he has only the haziest comprehension. So we develop a manipulative as opposed to a theoretical way of doing things.

Regardless of the ideology involved, manipulation always erodes theory. Apparatchiks in Russia are not supposed to graft like councilmen in New Orleans, but they do. Policemen in New York City (and perhaps elsewhere) are supposed to live on their salaries while rendering protection and equal justice to all citizens, whether rich or poor. Practically, things are a little different, so different that the very word "protection" starts to mean something entirely new to a bookie or a brothel-keeper. When he pays "protection" to a cop, it's not the protection *of* the law that he wants, but protection *from* the law. And where does this money go—watering, of course, many green pastures along the channels of the bureaucracy as it passes upward? It goes, of course, to politicians, who know, of course, where it comes from, but "don't know, don't want to know, don't want anyone to tell them."

Deplorable as it undoubtedly is, and productive of an entire elaborate machine of political lying, it's hard to see "normal" corruption as a wholly insidious practice. Organizational charts are ideal constructs, and in their practical operation, some allowance has to be made for the fact that people can't predict everything—or, indeed, much of anything. So the ideal structure has to be modified by little, practical, greasy "adjustments." Going literally by the rules (as some labor unions know very well) is an almost sure prescription for bringing any organization to a grinding halt. Whatever the form of organization, there are bound to be formal and informal, manipulative and theoretical procedures; and some form of corruption, therefore lying, seems an indispensable way of bringing the two elements into practical balance. If it's only buying Miss Whipplethorpe an expensive bottle of perfume for Christmas, the principle of duplicity is present. What begins as oil to reduce friction at crucial points of a transaction becomes an entire greasy machine, operating within the framework of an ideal structure, but supplanting it, eating out every last vestige of its actuality. So there is the dilemma. For purely practical reasons we can't live without some form of corruption and consequently of lying; if we have any sensitivity, we can't live with the consequences of unlimited lying and corruption; and if we have some way of coping with the problem (apart from periodic "vice-crusades" and reform movements which never fail to leave matters exactly where they were before), nobody has come up with it yet. The big ideological liar simply carries matters a step further by asserting, in the teeth of mere empirical reality, that the scheme is operating exactly the way it's structured to do—and terrorizing or throttling or murdering anyone who says different. The liberal ideology has, of course, its counterpart lie, that in a bourgeois democracy every man has just one vote, and that a majority of votes decides policy. What's ignored here—perhaps blandly rather than brutally, but no less effectually for that—is plutocracy's erosion from within of the republican scheme of liberty, equality, and (that vague parody of the Holy Ghost) fraternity. Whatever his creed, the modern ideologist, i.e., politician, exists only by virtue of a deliberate distance from reality, whether defined as idealism or paranoia. Assuming the alternatives are equivalent, let us therefore turn from the uninspiring topic of free-form lying to the more intriguing subject of lying under pressure or compulsion—where a variety of splendid examples lie immediately to hand.

But first there is an intermediate form to get out of the way—a variety of free-form yet compulsive lying, which could be called the myth of total consistency. For some reason, political spokesmen seem generally to feel that there is something humiliating or disgraceful about the act of changing one's mind, even in response to changed circumstances. An administration which alters course 180 degrees overnight will feel compelled to declare, yet without any evident compulsion, that its policy is really unaltered. Yesterday deflation of the currency was out of the question, today it is an established fact, yet our policy has not changed a fraction of a degree. A partial explanation of this seemingly gratuitous behavior may be the fear that someone will charge vacillation or even perhaps error. So instead of saying what is clearly true, "We tried one tack, it didn't work, so now we're trying the other," a fictitious and cumbersome consistency has to be imposed. This fuzzy fabrication takes place, not only with regard to short-term shifts of stance, where inconsistency might fairly be charged, but also in matters of long-term attitude, where a modicum of change might be excused as a modest indication of mental activity. The proper politician will not admit that he has changed his mind about anything whatever since he was twenty-three years old—preferring to seem stupid but monolithic rather than intelligent but variable. There is an obvious practical rationale behind this option: the political liar wants to impress on his public what he "stands for." Much better that they should identify him with a single, unchanging stance, than consider him a clever, shifty thinker, now on this side of a question, now on that. At the same time, he sharply increases his freedom of maneuver by making clear that just because he "stands for" something is no legitimate reason to suppose that he will do it. The more flagrant and gratuitous the contrast between profession and performance, the better. Any man may be impeded from carrying out his intentions by circumstances beyond his control—it is a perfectly legitimate excuse, but wholly undistinctive, and its energies extend hardly at all beyond the present moment. But when a politician constantly professes his intention of doing one thing, and then ostentatiously does the opposite, even while renewing his professions, the citizen can draw only one conclusion, that the subject is beyond his understanding. Planting this conclusion in his mind will doubtless lead to fruitful applications in the future—applications which will make themselves automatically, and without further effort on the part of the political virtuoso.

By "lying under pressure" I do not of course mean lying under oath, since the oath, with its tired formula

"so help me God" has no real meaning, and adds little
or nothing to the pressure bearing on the prospective
liar. He does not seriously expect God to help him in
any case; the only thing he's really afraid of is the laws
against perjury, and they are neither a clear nor a present danger. Divine retribution is nothing but a joke,
and a joke in rather poor taste. But practical alternatives are hard to devise. Someone has suggested that
the oath-taker might well propose his own penalty for
his own perjury, in the event of its being proved on
him. Fine and imprisonment would be the modest
suggestions of a man not very confident of his own
truthfulness, and not entitled to much credit; one who
offered himself to mutilation or lingering and painful
death might well be believed, especially if he had before him the example of a couple of fellows who had
proposed this penalty and actually had it inflicted on
them. A good deal more serious reflection might go
into this decision than into reciting the present perfunctory formula. At the very least, one might suggest
that the penalty for perjury should never be less than
double the penalty for the actual crime under discussion, since merely prudential considerations make it
natural for a man to lie when he has much to gain and
little to lose. And the meaningless formula of the oath,
suggesting that all a man has to lose by perjury is God's
favor, amounts—God save the mark—to an open invitation that he should lie under oath whenever he
thinks he can get away with it.

But since pressure is not defined, these days, by the

favor of God, nor yet by anxiety over one's immortal soul, it must be measured in practical terms. Evidently it is calculated in money, social standing including loss of public office and influence—and of course in the formal penalties annexed to getting caught. Perhaps the haziness of these various overlapping jurisdictions is what makes political lying so convenient that it can happen almost by accident. For it isn't simply that standards are lax, but that they are indefinite, unpredictable. On the one hand, only the minutest fraction of the political lies told under oath ever get detected; and only a minim of those ever get prosecuted or punished. On the other hand, merely being questioned about certain matters may entail significant penalties, without any sort of formal conviction or legal conclusion. Yet even conviction, if one's misdeeds are heinous enough to have excited, I won't say the public but the media, may yield immense rewards—contracts, interviews, serial rights, fame and fortune. Since no man can really predict what the reward or penalty is going to be for his particular untruth (public life being like the lottery in Babylon in this respect), lying under pressure becomes a prudential calculation involving the usual variables: maximum gains, minimum losses, the analysis of peripheral advantages and disadvantages. This is very different from the way things used to be when the only serious judge in these matters was omnipotent and omniscient, and the great penalty involved nothing less than an eternity of hell. Under the new circumstances of our day, one could hardly fail to anticipate that great progress would be made in the art of political lying under pressure.

Nothing shows more strikingly the advances made in the art than a changed status of the old maxim that when lying under pressure, one should fabricate as little as possible, weaving one's lies indistinguishably into a fabric of truth. The whole scale of modern lying seems to have gone beyond this sort of petty needlepoint—which was appropriate enough as long as the aim of lying was to convince, but which became obsolete when the purpose of lying was to confuse and bewilder. Under these new circumstances, the more lies, contradictions, anomalies, and absurdities one can produce, and the more thickly they are layered atop one another, the better the whole strategy works. Instead of adding up to a convincing picture, the lies should add up to total, multiform, chaotic disorder and confusion. The successful liar should intersperse his lies with frequent professions of ignorance or incomprehension. He is himself as muddled as the picture he paints—he has forgotten crucial details, he does not understand, he can't imagine, that's something he wouldn't like to speculate about, he doesn't know what a plain assertion means, and he does not recognize a flat contradiction in terms. He does not try to "make sense" of things; events in his story which look or sound very strange indeed have never stirred him to reflection. It's all too much for him; and this in trivial as well as important points, so that the very ideal of clear and coherent truth will be obscured. Especially useful in this practice is the technique of correcting one lie with another. The 1710 authors had some inkling of this device, but they thought of it only as a technique analogous to the setting of back-fires when the woods are ablaze. To combat A's lie, B would start one of his own. A respectable but primitive notion. The new device is for the same man to tell successive lies, by which he exhausts as well as exasperates the seeker after truth—for of course he never admits that either is a lie, or that there's the slightest contradiction between them. The new artist in political untruth is a veil-maker; behind every veil that seems to be lifted (yet it's never lifted so far or so fully that it ceases to blur the vision) lies another veil and yet another—the end of all is gauze, haze, and shadowy suspicion.

Suspicion is the keynote. The new politician swims in popular suspicion, and thrives on it, as Mao's guerilla swims in the ocean of the people. He does not shun suspicion, which has attached to it a kind of interest and attention, as of an open sore. Under the new dispensation, even if a politician knew some clear, specific fact favorable to himself, he might refuse to state it, since its very clarity and specificity would contrast unfavorably with the general haziness of his thought and style. What then gives the political liar his buoyancy? Why doesn't he sink through the mists of his own equivocation? One group of answers is clearly negative. Quarrelling with the new breed of politician is like attacking a cuttlefish; he will blacken and befoul the whole medium before you get to him. Since every-

thing he says is evasive, ambiguous, or quickly con-
tradicted, since he hides behind shoals of "spokesmen"
who can be disavowed whenever that proves convenient, and since he is unscrupulous about inventing his
own rules and deciding which of the laws he will obey,
there is little chance of dragging him out from behind
his inkscreen. A liar of this sort does well, therefore, to
get himself a preliminary reputation as an ugly, vindictive, and treacherous customer; and in doing this, it is
particularly advantageous that he show himself indis-
criminate as between friend and foe. For example, a
man whose fitness for office is being questioned
should not waste his time arguing that he really is fit
for office. Rather, he should move at once to blacken
the name of his intimate associate and necessary suc-
cessor in the event of removal from office, thus letting
the argument make itself: "if X is removed, we will get
G, who is just as bad, if not worse." Equally to be
commended is the practice of deliberately neglecting,
when under question, some crucial functions of one's
office, which will result in gross harm to the aged, the
poor, the sick, and the helpless. Blame for the damage
to this pathetic group can then be laid on those who are
inquiring into one's misdeeds. If only the policeman
did not, by his harrassment, keep the criminal so busy
defending himself, that worthy fellow would have
more time to distribute chocolate bonbons to needy
newsboys.

On a more positive note, the new liar (I mean, of
course, the new-style liar, since one can count on his

being far from a neophyte at the art) will be well advised to avoid the sullen and reluctant note in the act of prevarication itself. He may avoid speaking at all for as long as he can; he may issue guarded and devious statements on his own. But under interrogation, the new principles suggest, it is his business to be buoyant, inventive, profuse, and preferably condescending to his interrogators. The alternative procedure is not without its merits, to be sure. Everyone must recognize the possible advantages of trying to bore one's interrogators to death—the drab, tired response, the minimal perfunctory comment, the tedious juggling of terms. All very good as far as they go; but in using them, the fact that one lies under constraint (in several senses of the word) is all too apparent. For distracting and tantalizing effect, the smirk and the brassy air of confidence are much better. In the past, they were avoided on the grounds that they antagonize—a fatal flaw in logic. One who is committed to flagrant lying is bound to antagonize, and he should take advantage of that fact by denying his inquisitors (so far as possible) a chance to focus on the details of his fabrications. The defensive lie can be converted, by a simple process of multiplication, into an offensive maneuver. The liar should confess (whether sincerely or otherwise makes no difference) to flagrant, offensive, but non-criminal opinions whenever possible, should flaunt every red rag conceivable under the bull's nose, and thus distract and diffuse attention from more vital areas. There is always a danger in exercising craft from a defensive posture, or at least exercising it too openly, since it invites the exercise of counter-craft. Misguided innocence verging on stupidity is not only harder to attack, but more likely to win public sympathy. The new-style political liar combines frankness of manner carried to the point of effrontery with total vagueness about specifics, amounting if possible to an appearance of mental atrophy. One particular advantage of this procedure appears in the matter of collective lying, where it used to be possible to check one man's story against another's. This is far more difficult when both men tell confused and incoherent stories, which are not even internally consistent.

Division of labor is thus a first principle of modern political lying. Each man contributes his mite to a structure aimed not at inspiring conviction but at preventing it. The true beauty of the scheme is that it doesn't have to produce a story which is rational, rationalized, or rationalizable. As soon as one accepts universal suspicion, in the absence of proof positive, as an optimum condition, a great weight falls from one's shoulders. It is the weight of explaining or understanding the course of events or the pattern of facts which one casts on the interrogators. By saying "I don't know," one can gain at a stroke the immense advantage of the negative argument; one is aligned automatically with the non-manipulators; and, having so little responsibility to tell a coherent tale, one can invent the more fecklessly within one's specific purview. A modest measure of contempt and loathing go along with the suspicion one is bound to generate; but what of that? The very concept of "politician" already carries an aroma of these feelings; to be the special focus of them suggests immediately that one is eminent in one's chosen line. For greatness is a quality of soul, and makes itself felt in charlatanry and imposture as well as in any of the other professions.

Proximity lends a kind of specious grandeur to recent American liars on the political scene. Indeed, one can't wholly ignore an administration during which the president, vice-president, and attorney general were all exposed as gross and flagrant public frauds—not to mention a shoal of lesser fry, whose names won't stand even in the lower ranks of infamy, with Pigott, Esterhazy, and Albert B. Fall. The more eminent Nixonites are eminent in the natural history of political lying chiefly for negative reasons. They lied, not simply from greed (though indeed they were swinishly greedy), not from malice or fear (though they were certainly malicious and fearful men), not even from a natural though corrupt love of the lie itself. The lie was bigger than any of them, than all of them; they didn't create it, it created them. They lied, it would seem, automatically, mechanically, out of teamwork, like the man who went to hell simply from reluctance to break up a good party. Of course the piecework system took its own sort of revenge. The interweaving of lies became intricate beyond the power of any individual to master it; hence the overriding fear that any odd loose thread might lead to an unravelling of the whole enterprise; hence the attempt to stonewall by denying, however absurdly, every last, least imputation. If they hadn't lied so desperately about trivialities, hardly anyone would have suspected them of monstrosities. What they tried to create by their multiple protestations was, at best, confusion; what in fact they created was an absolute if unspecific conviction that within that inky cloud of gibberish there must lurk a particularly disgusting cuttlefish. As, indeed, there proved to be—a whole tentacular, sucker-equipped family of them. But here we enter on a topic far too elaborate and in every direction as far as the eye can see too nasty to be dwelt on:

> Misericordia e giustizia gli sdegna:
> Non ragionam di lor, ma guarda e passa.

Dirty Stuff

To think of the obscene brings us onto a wider stage. Suppose we say, for starters, that the obscene is a word or act that causes a particular response; virtually everybody will recognize what that response is, though agreement on what does or doesn't cause it will be harder to come by, and a few people will say that it shouldn't exist at all—that outrage is itself an outrageous response to anything whatever. Very likely if one could find a society without any customs at all, it would be impervious to the sense of obscenity. But this is a highly metaphysical speculation. Within human society as we know it, the obscene is a shock rupture of ingrained social codes controlling verbal or physical action. By "ingrained" social codes I mean those to which moral value is attached, as opposed to merely convenient observances like driving on the right side of the road. The particulars don't much mat-

ter. Our heavy codes have mainly to do with sex and
excretion, and we automatically think of the obscene
in these connections. But among some South American tribes, where sex and excretion are completely
open, the behavioral codes center on food, and the
obscene would be to waste a piece of spider-monkey
or eat a steak of snake. As a rule, perpetrators of the
obscene should be aware of the codes they are violating. An innocent (an infant, an animal, a person from
an alien culture) can hardly be obscene in violating a
code he doesn't recognize or care about. Perhaps
there's an element of the parochial in most judgments
of obscenity—as when oriental men think western
women grossly provocative because they don't hide
their faces under a yashmak, while western men think
oriental women slyly provocative because they do.
There's not much question that we can train out of
ourselves most of the reactions that inspire the word
"obscene"; not much question, either, that if we grope
around in almost anyone at the limits of what he thinks
tolerable, we will find a little area—conditional,
limited, and perhaps shamefaced—where the word
seems to apply.

In the normal course of events, most of us live in a
variety of environments that require us to adjust our
definitions of the obscene from minute to minute and
circumstance to circumstance. A word or gesture
that's perfectly natural on the waterfront will be scandalous in a convent. Tact is the art of commanding this
distance between decorum and the obscene, of quietly

avoiding obscenity when we don't want it and deftly achieving it when we do. Two variants of obscenity which take for themselves a recognized target can be seen to flank and define our proper topic: the blasphemer directs his outrage specifically against the deity and his laws; the perpetrator of foul insult directs it against an enemy, individual or collective. Obscenity itself, lying in the uncommitted middle range of bad-mouthing, is the least sharply focused of the options. It may turn outward against public mores, or inwardly, against one's own inhibitions and conventions. A pure, natural setting is the moment when one has just missed a nail, but not one's thumb, with a hammer. The moment is explosive. The pain, outrageous and sudden, requires some release; the fault is entirely one's own; there is nobody to be hit back; one explodes against an interior curtain of verbal repression, as if to answer the pain with a like violence. The curse somehow gets you even.

Because there is guilty pleasure in the obscene—pleasure associated with actions, with words as the symbols of actions, and with the idea of breaking taboos which forbid both words and actions—exercising this pleasure could hardly help becoming a game, and purveying it to the passive a business. In both forms, the obscene obviously takes on new nonexpressive motivations—virtuosity and display in the first instance, calculation in the second. An artist in foul speech (I think particularly of an Arkansas corporal who put me through basic training at Jefferson Barracks in 1943) aims only to surpass himself. His goal is glory, to be known as the man with the most filthy, ingenious tongue in camp. (From a severely practical point of view, high artistry of this order is sometimes self-defeating: men perform monkey-drill much better when they are not torn between awe at a rocket-barrage of cursing, and silent, convulsive laughter at the sheer skill of it.) As for obscenity as a business, I suppose one of its main considerations is to promise as much and give as little as possible. Calculating the point where this minimum crosses that maximum is an activity with an interest of its own—game-playing indeed, but not at all like the game played by my corporal, for whom giving and getting were in some way synonymous. In general, the relation of commercial pornography to the spontaneously obscene seems comparable to the relation between military discipline and human bravery; yet there's no way to be elitist about the matter. However grubby the product of the porno-bookstore, however tired and mechanical the tart, the patron of both finds release for a part of himself that he knows and despises. He is a swine, well, he will find some pig to wallow with for a while. We are only now learning in what close, complementary bonds the Victorian angel in the house was linked with the Victorian whore in the lane.

In his appropriation and debasement of the obscene within his client, the commercial exploiter confronts a difficulty analogous to that faced by the solemn analyst of obscenity, the obscenologist, as it were. The latter's

edifying scientific intentions corrupt and simultaneously sanitize, despite his worst intentions, the examples that he cites. Even when he picks up words like
"shit" and "fuck" for inspection, he touches them only
with gleaming, stainless-steel forceps (represented on
the still-sanitary page by quotation marks), in a solemn
clinical atmosphere, the very reverse of the exceptional
rage and disgust which usually authenticate such
words. I must apologize, before anything else, for such
artificiality, which forces me, in typing out polite, dis-
cursive obscenity, to commit counter-obscenities, for
which I can plead no excuse but necessity. Among
other admirable rules laid down in "The Revo-
lutionist's Handbook and Pocket Companion" by
John Tanner, M.I.R.C. (it is an appendix to Shaw's
Man and Superman) is one for corporal punishment of
the young, which proposes that one should never beat
a child except in uncontrollable rage. Obscenity in its
cleanest form, least contaminated by prudence or
exhibitionism or self-interest, is similarly the expression of pure, incoherent passion; but passion in explosive, i.e., contained-liberated form.

The conditions, it will be observed, are double. If
there is no suppression of caged, explosive feelings,
there will be little or no obscenity, though there may
be a lot of other things; if the taboos aren't violated
deliberately and antagonistically, there will be little
sense of obscenity, either expressive or responsive.
Like wit, with which its alliance is ancient and intimate, obscenity frees a reality principle within us that

has been clamoring to get out. It cuts through layers of social artifice and aspiration, reducing us to the gut and groin that we inescapably are and know ourselves to be, despite incessant prodding to be otherwise. Obscenity may or may not purify, but it releases; on the other hand, it also incites, and like many stimulants seems to demand more and more violent satisfactions. Whether it's a therapy or a sickness remains a bit ambiguous.

In any case, the obscene is a breaking open, a breaking out, a countering of norms and surfaces imposed by society or our societally-conditioned selves. If it is not *against,* it is nothing. For each nation, the debris points to the weapon of destruction, and vice versa. Of all peoples, the French, whose training in their polite speech is toward the sparse, formal, and lucid, are most given to Rabelaisian profusion in their obscenity. Eugène Robert's massive *Dictionnaire des injures,* though ostensibly devoted to the art of insult, includes an immense array of general obscenities, offering to the verbal duellist or displayman an incredible range of alternatives and optional combinations. (Cartesian duality is carried to almost parodic lengths by French dictionaries of *argot,* with their scholastically precise distinctions between innumerable words implying different varieties and tonalities of whores, pricks, and asses.) By contrast, the Spaniard, whose normal speech includes a good deal of the ceremonious and whose pride in family is legendary, often conveys his ultimate obscene sentiment with a gesture of the head and a curt, contemptuous phrase—"*Tu madre*," thy mother. *Not* saying the operative word seems a particularly devious and deadly form of obscenity, since it forces the victim to contaminate his own mind, to call up the expression that the speaker does not even deign to voice. In an equivalent way, the Italian forces into violent conjunction the two poles of his moral outrage in the expletive, "*Porca madonna*"; and the German, whose values are cleanliness, efficiency, and order, almost always expresses his sense of the obscene with the scatological. But the Japanese, for whom almost every aspect of life is or can be holy, have almost no special language for obscenity. Ladies who are not only respectable but distinguished, and in situations of perfect decorum, will use words which are the equivalent of "shit" and "fuck"—only in those circumstances they aren't of course in any way equivalent. Japanese insult apparently includes a few mild comparisons with animals, but nothing that we would recognize as artistic or inventive vituperation.

Negatively as well as positively, the power of the taboo to determine the obscenity is almost absolute: where taboos are strong, obscenity clusters; where they are weak, it hardly forms up at all. When women were swathed in yards of dry-goods, veils, boas, crinolines, and high collars, the glimpse of an ear or an ankle was titillating, a word like "bloomers" occasioned embarrassed laughter, and even the pianos had limbs instead of legs. The power of the taboo to create an obscene meaning out of whole cloth was nicely illustrated by a little red book of *Mother Goose Censored,* which circulated during the 1930's:★

> Peter, Peter, pumpkin eater,
> Had a wife and couldn't ████CENSORED████ her;
> He put her in a pumpkin shell,
> And there he ████CENSORED████ her very well.

Swift said it: "A clean-minded man is a man of nasty ideas."

In an essay no less interesting for being demonstrably wrong, Stendhal linked the downfall of the comic to the advent of government by bicameral legislature. His argument was that the comic was funny only by contrast with an accepted standard of the noble and dignified. Under democracy, what used to be automatically ludicrous is simply another seriously discussable way of pursuing happiness. The only argument against this diagnosis is historical: things simply haven't worked out that way. The comic, instead of disappearing, has changed nature. Its definition has widened and shifted, it has become more argumentative, more explanatory, perhaps more invidious. The pure comedy of manners, exemplified by "Le bourgeois gentilhomme," is indeed obsolete. Even the title is effectually untranslatable today, for it harbors three hideously difficult enigmas which for the seven-

★The bibliographical circumstances of this splendid spoof are odd and elaborate. It was published in 1929 by "Mother Goose" from her temporary residence at 100 Fifth Avenue, New York City; Knopf reprinted it in 1930, and one Kendall Banning held copyright.

teenth century simply didn't exist: what's a bourgeois? what's a gentleman? and why is the combination of the two concepts absurd, therefore funny? True, we can still exploit contrasts of manners onstage, but without the gaiety, the assurance, the true comic distance that come from an unquestioned single set of values. Instead of comedy, which doesn't care about anything, we start to get satire and sentiment, which do.

In somewhat the same way, the obscene depends on the primal energy of the sacred—maybe not altogether, but for a lot of its energy. When there is no immediate general recognition of the sacred, or when the sacredness of the sacred has to be explained—even controverted—it seems likely the spontaneously, joyfully obscene will get heavier, more sullen, even morally calisthenic.

For some centuries in the western world, a naked woman appearing publicly in lubricious attitudes has been thought obscene. We note how burlesque, which began as low parody of the classic myths, shaded gradually and by natural affinity into a sex-show, one sort of anti-statement leading into another. But recently, if the echoes I hear from off-Broadway are to be trusted, the naked woman is not only an expected figure, a convention, her whole import has changed. She is an emblem of honesty, frankness, moral ventilation-with-sanitation, and a standing reproach to the audience, shrinking prudishly in the symbolic dark under their dishonest and hypocritical vestments. If she is not always an example to be instantly followed (audiences have been known to accept the cue, and disrobe completely for a communal nudist frolic), she nonetheless authenticates and validates the show. Whether all this authenticity is really authentic or just a pretext for something else is a point that could be argued; indeed, it has to be argued, if only *in foro conscientiae*. How little moral pretext suffices to sanitize an exhibition the patent aim of which is to titillate? I suppose it depends on how gross a hypocrite one wants to consider oneself. It is a remarkably open-ended question.

But the peripheral point is almost as important. If the naked and sexually enticing woman is an emblem of moral rectitude, the effect of obscenity, if we're going to have such an effect onstage at all, will have to be achieved in some other way—by intercourse on stage, simulated or real, preferably with one or several of the variations that are still recognized as perversions. (I know, "perversion" as a term implies a parochial attitude toward sexual behavior; but if there are no real perversions, an audience must be persuaded that it is watching one—something special—if it is to be stirred out of its ho-hum attitude toward the conventional.) Inflation works upon symbols of the obscene as upon the fiscal symbols: the higher the numbers, the lower the value of the unit.

Literary obscenity is of course all simulated, designed to create, by art or craft, a verbal equivalence of a social or psychological event. The equivalence is two-directional; the artist is bound not only to communicate an experience, but to do so within or against the verbal mores of his culture—mores which may provide only inadequate verbal counters for saying what he wants to say. There are linguistic media within which a number higher than five can only be represented as "many"; cultures which are deaf to many of our cherished overtones, as we are deaf to theirs. Within our own linguistic tradition there are many areas that used to be lively and vivid, but which are now dead and literally buried—old metaphors worn to triteness, images sunk so deeply in formulas that we no longer feel them as images at all, entire stories rubbed down to a fleeting formulaic phrase—as when we speak of a prodigal son or a good Samaritan. Time and constant usage wear the sharp edges off locutions, as they do off coins. It would be ridiculous to suppose that the ordinary everyday conversation of the American army could be represented without the inevitable, monotonous, all-purpose adjective, "fuckin'." It is equally ridiculous to suppose that such usage represents anything obscene in the sense of verbal outrage. Quite the contrary; the word is a routine social convention, a filler on the order of "Y'know," spoken more out of habit and perhaps deliberate stupidity (to express, if anything, the nothingness of mass military existence) than out of any active feelings at all. With the idea of sexual intercourse it has nothing whatever to do. And when a novelist represents the speech of the army by reproducing this feature as it really occurs in daily life, the effect he gets is one of

drabness and dreariness, of violence become monotonous, routine, meaningless.

The burden of representing unspeakable outrage
falls inevitably on other expressions and devices when
"fuckin'" has been given the everyday, commonplace
function of a mild intensive like "very." In addition to
scraping up another and dirtier word (but no culture
possesses at any one time more than a limited supply of
these), a violation of sense and syntax, or the sheer
force of mechanical repetition, can be used to deepen
the impression of fury. The peremptory, disjointed,
spiteful sentences of Jason Compson are extraordinarily effective in developing the reader's feeling for an
absolutely cold and vindictive mind, though Faulkner
throughout *The Sound and the Fury* uses no expletive
more potent than "damn." Joyce has Private Carr re-
sort to the familiar ultimate word in the depths of the
Nighttown scene of *Ulysses,* emphasizing not only il-
logicality and mechanical repetition, but an eloquent
rhetorical rhythm as well: "I'll wring the neck of any
fucking bastard says a word against my bleeding fucking king." But this spirited and forceful declaration has
been carefully prepared for, by Joyce's meticulous
avoidance of the term during the first 580 pages of the
novel. The word has not been debased or rendered
habitual; its explosion here is a triumph of blind and
incoherent ferocity. Something, indeed, is to be said
for the sheer hammer-like repetition of a single word,
even though not in itself particularly violent. In his
classic study, *Lars Porsenna, or the future of swearing and*

improper language, Robert Graves cites a general offier operating under severe restrictions, who managed to convey deep sentiments about a slack member of an honor guard with the inspired sentence, "Oh, you naughty, *naughty,* NAUGHTY trumpeter!"

Language has many resources other than just vocabulary, and to a certain degree every author controls the range of his own verbal palette. If his scale is generally light throughout, he will have no difficulty finding dark tones where he needs them. But there is such a thing as a verbal climate, and it changes over the years, as do the spectrum of colors that our eyes are trained to see in paintings and the range of voices that we find gratifying in vocal music. (Constable taught his generation to see what green grass looks like; early oratorios and operas were sometimes scored for a couple of sopranos and a counter-tenor, leaving the lower register unrepresented altogether.) Verbal artists particularly are dependent for the basic materials of their work on the common linguistic heritage, the common linguistic habits. Apart from the colloquial patterns of his day, a writer lives in a tangible tradition of language, which has imposed value-laden connotations on words and concepts he is bound to use. He lives also in a haphazard but necessary linguistic projection ("What am I going to sound like fifty or a hundred years from now?") which is no less important to him for being hard to formulate unpretentiously. Especially when he finds many of the linguistic habits bequeathed or imposed by his culture to be repulsive, the writer has to guess for himself at an enduring dialect, one that will not sound mannered or effete, nor yet hokey in its contemporaneity, when read a few years hence. This is hard enough for ordinary prose, and worse when one is aiming at extreme effects; for horrible examples, consult the Gothic novels, the lending-library romancers of the early twentieth century, or the high erotic moments in the fiction of H. G. Wells.

In these tight, mysterious circumstances, gaining a single effect of pure, passionate, unlabored obscenity is no small task. Indeed, it calls for a measure of tact and intricate compromise, combined with inspired invention, to which only the combined talents of Danton and Talleyrand would be adequate. Imitating the surface of what your age considers obscene yields only the meager vocabulary and few gross images available to Studs Lonigan and his ilk. The inspired literary obscenity, fit to stand through the ages alongside Petronius, Rabelais, and Swift, will not be the work of a careless, unthinking moment. Rich as it is in linguistic filth, the spirit of the age cannot altogether suffice for the careful writer. He needs verve as well as squalor, high style as well as dirty stuff, and behind both of these a sense (at least potential) of elevation, to give relief to his spiritual landscape. The reader who has spent his reading day in a sewer can hardly bring a fresh response to what is, after all, just one more stink.

All too often in public discussions of obscenity, it's taken for granted that if we inhibit the rights of pornographers to ply their trade (in magazines, movies, over television), we're on the way to crushing the right of some starry-eyed artist of the future to use the same tonal values in the formulation of some indescribably beautiful chord. Something like this awful repression may, indeed, someday occur, though the scanner of horizons looks in vain for a cloud even as big as a man's hand. Be that as it may, there's patently a lot of cant and hypocrisy in the argument as constructed. The pimping pornographer who claims to be fighting the battles of some future Proust or Joyce doesn't deserve much of our sympathy. If there wasn't good hard cash to be turned from his pious pose, one would soon see how much he cared about Proust or Joyce, supposing he had heard of either.

Twisting the matter another way, it's perfectly arguable that letting down all the barriers of "decency" (I don't mean real decency, of course, since that can't be legislated; just conventions of proper public discourse) will pose more problems for the really creative artist than it solves. It renders flat and commonplace certain expressions that he may want to use for his strongest and most violent effects; if he chooses not to use them at all, the prevalent standard of taste imposes on him (perhaps unjustly) a fussy and old-maidish air. For better or worse—it's not really an arguable point—Dostoevsky moved the benchmarks from around Henry James; in the same way, the most risqué novels of the last thirty years are rendered pallid by *Last Exit to Brooklyn*. It's hard to stay out of the obscenity-sweepstakes, but each new success renders it harder to win. The diffusion of the obscene (which is just another consequence, I suppose, of the romantic spilling of the sacred) subjects artistic taste to an ultimate leveling and democratizing from which it's the constant endeavor of every artist to escape. He wants language of immediate distinction, carrying effortless impact; our liberals offer him the same rights as everybody else. It's a rotten bargain. The artist may get immunity from prosecution, but in contemporary society, this is hardly a significant immunity. No backwoods Alabama prosecutor is going to hound down Philip Roth (who reads Philip Roth in backwoods Alabama?) when he's got *Penthouse* and "Deep Throat" to exercise his publicity-gathering talents on. Besides, everybody knows that being banned in Boston is absolutely the most effective form of advertising, in Boston and elsewhere.

In short, the perils from which the artist is saved when we effectively eliminate a code-decision between the decent and the obscene are trifling, imaginary perils. What is imposed on him instead is a kind of schizoid uncertainty-anxiety about the verbal standards of his own days as contrasted with those of other days before and after, and of other cultures in other places. What serious literary artist wants to be caught up in a whirlpool of linguistic bad taste whipped up by the frantic effort of one freak to outdo another? I'm saying not that this has happened here and today, far less that the remedy is some form of bluenosed censorship, just that when a decaying puritanism begins to muddle the obscene with the sacred, directions get lost, along with a sense of where other folks are.

Lest these seem groundless warnings, consult the *Imitations* of Robert Lowell, where the violence of the poet's personal, contemporary voice is imposed (disastrously, to my taste) on the work of European poets working in different traditions, to different coordinates. Mr. Lowell isn't by any means unique in his translational manhandling (Louis Zukovsky has done worse by Catullus), but he allows his own voice, and his own linguistic values, to trample all over those of his authors. Too often the equivalents for traditional usages to which he resorts are not equivalents at all but harsh and violent substitutions. Maybe they are what the original author might have written had he been born and raised under Robert Lowell's circumstances (though a guess on that subject amounts to little more than a flying leap at the moon), but they are generally far distant from anything that the original authors wrote, being the persons they were.

The confusion of verbal values which Lowell's *Imitations* point up in a very limited way is general and pervasive. It grows, I think, from the ruin of an ancient set of hierarchical verbal values, and from their inversion. Watered down, homogenized, and stood on their heads, the sacred and the obscene have become so nearly indistinguishable that deliberate effort is required to set them apart. The grossest of pornographers talk in oily tones of "moral frankness" and "esthetic honesty" and "facing facts." The man who cultivates the obscene for its own sake and without any appended garbage about "redeeming social purpose" has a little better chance of coming off with the shreds of moral integrity—a little better but not much. This emulsifying of the two spheres is a primary reason why all general rules regarding obscenity are absurd nowadays. Perhaps in the old days when society thought it knew what it was talking about on this matter, codes were possible, even under certain aspects desirable: no more. In contemporary society, the very question of obscenity is obscene; to answer it with an affirmation or a denial is an act of bad faith. The less we raise it, the better off we are; and any code we could devise would inevitably be surrounded by so many special contexts, circumstances, and conditions for social pretense and legal manipulation, as to render it instantly a nose of wax.

In surrendering, as it recently did, its claim to define the obscene by a lack of redeeming social purpose, the Supreme Court clearly took one short step toward a healthy skepticism. Anyone can see that the obscene isn't necessarily less obscene because it's hitched to a moral lesson, any more than a whorehouse is nicer if one is introduced into it by a deacon. But that this leaves the "local community" (meaning thereby the ambitious local prosecutor and the leader of the local prude society) free to take on this intricate and exacting task of discrimination is little short of ludicrous. One looks forward with awe and amazement to the potential complications which the new arrangement of rules-and-no-rule can bring about. Will it be possible to prosecute a man for reading a dirty book in a plane occupying air-space over eastern Kansas? What recourse will the publisher of Baudelaire have against the city council of Ogallala, Nebraska? Won't the standard-setters for Podunk and Peoria actually have to read all the things they object to—a time-consuming and often a puzzling process?

But in fact these queries go a long way to suggest how, not unpleasantly, the new ruling is bound to work out. For by making censorship local, one makes it, more than ever, ineffectual; as with local prohibition, district ordinances are made to be circumvented or allowed to mildew. At the same time, the obscene retains its power as a concept, if only because one knows that Aunt Tillie in Dubuque isn't allowed to see the wicked flick one can catch oneself by travelling to Iowa City. Copies of *Ulysses* will cross state lines in plain brown wrappers, to the exultant pleasure of the reader, the profit of the under-counter purveyor, the advantage of the legal profession, and the mystification of the unco guid in the now morally purified community. Like jealousy and emulation, the obscene is triangular; we apply the word quite as much to what we think will outrage other people's moral standards as to what really and in fact offends our own. But the most promising prognosis of all is for a vast torpor and

weary indifference on the matter, which was surely
what the court anticipated when it shrugged and ut-
tered its Solomonic "Buh!"

Chaos and confusion are thus everybody's gain in
this new public policy on the obscene; or the Supreme
Court has at least given us a chance to test that
hypothesis. There promises to be much comedy and
little tragedy in its working out. But for the individual—on whom, as always, real responsibility rests
for thinking about the matter—the obscene remains
a sphinx in the path. An eighteenth-century arrangement of values (for which, personally, I feel much
sympathy) would request certain cleanly and com-
plete decorums, amounting almost to elegance, as
a condition of finding the obscene to be a willful and
aware violation of them. It's at least a nod in the direction of a Manichean outlook which seems to me as
close to optimism as modern man can safely come: a
throwback, if we can manage it, to the century of lights
with its equivalent darks. Here and there this spirit still
survives, perhaps with an access of larkiness, as I recently heard from friends who sublet their California
house for a year. Arriving to take possession, the ten-
ants presented themselves in full evening dress, somehow arranged or locally omitted to display their geni-
tals, which had, perhaps for the occasion, been gilded.
A little forced, no doubt, a bit *voulu;* but clearly in the
tradition of the *ancien régime.*

The nineteenth-century style is that of the *poète
maudit,* who plunges into the obscene as an adventure

in evil and a reaffirmation of spiritual law against mere nature. The great exemplar is of course Baudelaire, but one can find more than traces of the character in Swinburne, Poe, Huysmans, Sacher-Masoch. And for the twentieth century, the obscene represents an act of deep choice, an affirmation, even a creation, of the self. Far from being an occasional adventure, or a testing of alien moral values, it is itself in the character of moral nutriment. Through the obscene one declares one's independence of the rotten genteel tradition, and achieves the instant, universal *bona fides* of moral authenticity. I don't have to emphasize the element of fraud here, some actual and some potential, but the logic is all right. What happens when you look under the logic at the motivation is another matter.

Any time that the respectable (lumped all together in the accepted paranoid pattern) is felt to be patently obscene, then frank and deliberate violation of it is in order. Whatever else one may be rotting of (that, I repeat from my eighteenth-century stance, covers a lot of ground), it isn't inertia. How far one wants to push the formula that if I revolt against the faulty I'm bound to be faultless, depends very largely on one's balance between pretension and a sense of humor. The foul-mouthed saint-comedian-criminal-buffoon who is the characteristic moral register of our time (Genet, Céline, Lenny Bruce, et al.) seems to push and splinter the moral paradoxes as far as they will go; agile and elusive behind all his impersonations, he is unfailingly ready with Rousseau's all-purpose defense, which is

simply to confess everything, plus 20 percent for con-
tingencies, long before one is accused of it. He thus
gains the right, which he'll liberally exercise, to bad-
mouth the rest of us. Far from being obliged to suggest
ways we can improve ourselves, he's under major obligation not to. In this day of confrontation psychology, who can deny the value of confrontation obscenity, which elicits moral responses from us (maybe) by
affronting our moral values as cruelly, as corruptly, as
intimately as possible? Of course there's something
obscene, too, about having apparent moral dilemmas
too easily both ways—but that's a purely metaphorical
"obscene."

Without very much enthusiasm, then, I recognize
the style in obscenity of my age: it is moralistic and
confused. And without being able to account for the
preference very clearly, I affirm my own predilection
for esthetic clarity. I like my obscenity sharp and pure,
like a purple splotch across a canvas of Nicolas de Staël;
I don't want it doing me good underhandedly. One of
my excuses for this stance is that the esthetic seems a
less heavy judgment than the moral; less to defend, less
to attack, mobility not nobility. Setting one's own
style in the matter allows, it seems to me, a longer
perspective and a freer choice of the company in which
one chooses to be judged. That it's an evasion of sorts I
won't try to deny. Let him who will look straight and
hard, with an aroused moral conscience, at the full
range and scope of filth and dishonor in this world of
ours—the sketchiest recital of which would fill an en-

cyclopedia, blacken the heavens, and earn me a place among the obsessed and monomaniacal. Human kind, says the poet (or at least a bird, speaking to the poet), cannot bear very much reality. Whatever our pious truthtellers pretend, the obscene, when taken at its full valency, is a topic to be looked at askance, under peril of a scorched retina.

Beauty is only skin-deep, but ugly is to the bone.
—*Old saying, courtesy of Alice Sachs*

Ideas of Ugly

Like the obscene, the ugly is an unmistakable reaction
with a lot of questionable causes. Ancient wisdom tells
us that *de gustibus non est disputandum,* an adage that
hasn't cut short either disputes or discussions. But in a
cosmopolitan culture, esthetic relativism is the easiest
of all positions, and thrives on its own established
clichés. Ubangi tribesmen admire enlarged, platter-
like lips, and the natives of Tabar, off New Ireland,
fatten their wives, like Strasbourg geese, to a state of
delectable, globular rotundity. We think these anatom-
ical exaggerations ugly, the societies involved consider
them at least acceptable, perhaps admirable, maybe
beautiful; therefore judgments of the ugly are as diverse and as subjective as judgments of the beautiful,
the only constant is an opposition between them. Mul-
tiply examples, as it's easy to do, and one doesn't come
out far from the central principle of the only full-scale

treatise of the ugly, the 1853 *Aesthetik des Hässlichen* by a pupil of Hegel's, Karl Rosenkranz: "Wäre die Schöne nicht, so wäre das Hässliche gar nicht, denn es existirt nur als die Negation desselben."★

It's my impression that the dialectic carries a good deal of the argument in Rosenkranz's ringing but questionable declaration. As we've seen "die Schöne" isn't a single concept capable of being considered as a real existence, it's a rather watery abstraction from a lot of observed and loosely conglomerated particulars. More significantly, it isn't necessarily opposed to "das Hässliche," or vice versa. We have no reason to think that the Ubangi consider young people with unenlarged lips to be ugly, any more than we consider girls without makeup or modish clothes to be ugly, though we do indeed think they'd look better with a little styling. Besides, it's not at all clear that in the cases of enlarged lips or fat wives (which can stand for thousands of others), we're dealing with exclusively esthetic considerations. Religious beliefs and taboos, utilitarian considerations, and social values enter in; the fatness of the wife may be a social advertisement of wealth and leisure, as among the Chinese long fingernails and bound feet used to serve as marks of ostentatious uselessness. Worse still for the "negation" theory, there are instances where the ugly and the beautiful are so closely interwoven as to be almost

★"If there were no beauty, there would be no ugly at all, for the latter exists only as a negation of the former."

inseparable. Many snakes and some spiders, for example, are regarded with simultaneous loathing and admiration; loathing, not necessarily learned from society or grounded in theology, strong enough to make
women scream when they confront a serpent, admiration strong enough to make the same women welcome
the same serpents as motifs in jewelry. I should myself
find no contradiction between thinking a pile of offal
ugly in the street and a painting of it beautiful, on the
wall of a museum. There's a good deal of so-called
"motel" art which strives so hard to be pretty that we
respond to it instinctively as hideous.

The truth is that both "the beautiful" and "the ugly"
represent nothing but loose clusters of qualities, originally only partly esthetic in character. The antelope,
the jet plane, the leopard, a Brancusi sculpture all
have a sleek, polished efficient look that's one ingre-
dient going into "the beautiful"; the hyena, the car-
graveyard, the cockroach, and the nightmares of Hier-
onymus Bosch probably qualify with most people as
examples of "the ugly." But as there are many forms
of beautiful other than the sleek, so there are many
forms of ugly other than the dirty and distorted. The
second-rank adjectives under the beautiful point us
toward some of the many qualities that get lumped together in the final hazy abstraction: for example, radiant, sweet, gracious, pretty, majestic, harmonious,
dazzling, delicate, regular, and well-proportioned.
Under the ugly we find words like foul, shapeless, deformed, squalid, course, gross, clumsy, grotesque,

nasty, and distorted. These aren't my free associations operating unchecked, they are a selection from
the cornucopia of terms listed under "beautiful" and
"ugly" by Roget's celebrated *Thesaurus*. And it's
perfectly clear that when you spread out the components like this, there are some cross-compatibles; a
cloud could be shapeless and radiant, a giant majestic
and deformed, features delicate and distorted. It's also
true that each group contains incompatibles; it's hard
to be both majestic and delicate, shapeless and distorted. Yet, looking at the groups as wholes, it isn't
hard to see the two or three ideas of which each is
composed, or the rationale behind their unification in a
loose category, which is all that, at bottom, the notions
of "beautiful" and "ugly" amount to.

One can't look into Roget without further sensing
that the two categories are constantly used to define
one another; the beautiful is the undeformed and so
forth, the ugly is the uncomely and so forth. But here I
think there's a whole range in the degrees to which
one's response to either category depends on awareness of the other. I certainly don't recognize a pretty
girl by comparing her, consciously or unconsciously,
with an ugly one; my response to a litterpile or a
sludge-pool doesn't involve any very immediate juxtaposition with images of potential loveliness. Yet the
Beast is specially ugly as the potential lover of Beauty;
and the ugliness of a pack of hyenas tearing apart an
antelope is heightened by its counterpointing the victim's grace and agility. Evidently, when the ugly and

beautiful aren't in immediate contrast, our cultural values sometimes mediate between them, standing in for the one in the presence of the other. For instance, our tremendous cultural emphasis on cleanliness and the sanitary heightens, if it doesn't create, our almost religious horror of filth, excrement, and slimy things that make us feel, as we say, "squeamish." We don't need any specific beauty to contrast with the squalid; our sanitized standards of the cleanly, the seemly, and the beautiful will make the contrast by themselves. Thus it's hard to get rid once and for all of Herr Rosenkrantz's dialectic, however cobwebby; because if one looks for it, there's no beauty without a counterpart ugly somewhere, and vice versa. The way to get rid of it, if one doesn't find the dialectic useful, is experiential, not logical.

Right here, the ugly is crucial. We can easily widen our ability to see beauty outside our own cultural traditions; Benin bronzes, Persian miniatures, prehistoric cave-paintings, Noh-theater, African body-painting, Nazca pottery, Mycenean bronzes, and Papuan fetishes—there's nothing so remote in the cultural life of man, that the museum-culture of our times won't accept it gladly. In addition, cultural relativism (which shades indistinguishably into cultural uncertainty, thus into cultural inflation) renders many people tolerant of scandalous amateurism and barefaced ineptitude in the arts. Thus we can not only adapt, like chameleons, to anything, whether we understand its esthetic coordinates and objectives or not; having got used to admiring the emperor's new clothes, we can tell one new wardrobe from another, and discourse with learned awe on the subtle nuances separating this zero from that. Only the ugly remains a real test of discrimination.

I think this is most apparent in the striking instance of modern music, where the patter of polite applause that greets every new atonal horror may indeed conceal the presence of a few musicians who understand and genuinely appreciate what they're applauding—but which comes for the most part from people who find what they have heard to be hideous and incomprehensible, but are ashamed to say so. The Dada artists in their early days used to distribute, to patrons entering the gallery, axes with which to vent their uncontrollable fury on the art-objects; it would be a genuinely dangerous experiment in a modern concert hall.

To say that a work of art is ugly, repellent, and therefore of little value is a difficult, if not an impossible judgment to enunciate these days, when pleasing is the last and least of art's aims. Yet it's a legitimate point that if a work of art is so unpleasant that it causes us to turn away or think of something else, simply shutting the eyes of the mind to it, there's a fault somewhere, and it isn't necessarily in the eye or ear of the beholder. The tacit proposition that the work of art is a test for the discriminating, so that the more people it repels along the way, the higher is the distinction of the few survivors, has been milked for about all it's worth.

"It's good for you, dear," the nurse used to say as she swabbed on the iodine; "the more it hurts, the better it is." The words could be inscribed in fire over the entries to many an art gallery, many a concert hall.

The sense that one can't object to art as ugly grows out of the prevalence, indeed the incorporation, of the ugly *in* art. And this trend seems, in turn, to grow from a feeling, too widespread to be an affectation, that the world *is* essentially ugly, that to show it as anything else is to falsify it intolerably. This is a change in degree, if not in kind, from traditional uses of the ugly in art, where it served, in dutiful obedience to Herr Rosenkranz's formula, as foil or counterpoint to a specific beauty that overshadowed, or rather, overlighted it. Everyone will recall the way in which paintings of the Last Judgment or the Temptation of Saint Anthony, or a poem like the *Divine Comedy,* make ugly serve the ends of beauty. Medieval and Renaissance painters generally make as hideous as possible the faces of Christ's tormentors, by way of contrasting them with the meek benevolence of the Savior. In the Saint Anthony's particularly one feels occasionally that the macabre and the hideous have become matters of fascination in themselves, and the saint is no more than a pretext. But his presence nonetheless serves to frame and control the ugly, giving it a context of spiritual meaning as certainly as the structure of a Gothic cathedral orders the grotesque gargoyles and the rude, rowdy carvings under the choir-seats. Traditionally, a spot of the ugly serves to authenticate that beauty which negates it. "Justice made me, and eternal love" is part of the motto that Dante found written over Hell-gate; it implies that Hell is also beautiful precisely in its ugliness—that if seen as part of an immense whole, it is exactly suited to its function in a universe which can only make over all for beauty and beneficence. Sir Thomas Browne, who also was fond of long perspectives, tells us that nothing is ugly except chaos, everything else being deliberately shaped by the Creator and bearing the mark of His sublime art.

Since Dante wrote, the ugly has slowly and subtly wormed its way out of the subordinate role to which he so firmly assigned it. The appropriately encyclopaedic study of the process will doubtless have much to tell us of why German and Germanic artists seem to have had such a particular affinity for the nightmarishly ugly. It will point up the slow seepage of the unchallenged ugly into the inferior genres—caricature, capriccios, grotesque decorations, comic subplots. Deep ugly crops up only here and there at first. DeFlores, the protagonist of Middleton's *The Changeling* is so ugly he can hardly think of anything else; but when Beatrice-Joanna comes to know him, she finds to her astonishment that he is even uglier than that, ugly down to the very core of his heart. Charles Bovary's hat, Flaubert tells us, had depths of ugliness, like an imbecile's face; that wretched schoolboy hat is an emblem of Charles's misbegotten and clumsily patched-up self, and everything we learn about him throughout the book only deepens this sense of ugliness (not evil, not pathos, nothing natural, nothing corrupt, just dense, sluggish ugliness)—so that in the end, that hat becomes a paradigm of the novel itself, within which only the crassest sort of vulgarity can flourish.

At what point do we feel the ugly, not merely asserting its independence of beauty, but its predominance over it? Not, I think, in grotesques or fantasies or even adventures in the macabre, like Gothic novels and related forms of diablerie; in their very separateness and willful quality, these forms still pay tribute to the positives they negate. But the morbidly fascinating, which rose into prominence as a theme with romanticism, in good part as a specific sequel to the Byronic pose, carried within it the germs of the revolution if not the revolution. Here our historian will find himself treading in the footsteps of Professor Mario Praz, whose *Romantic Agony* chronicles many stages and variations at which we need do no more than gesture here. A first formulation, that extremes of pleasure merge with extremes of pain, led to a further implication that without extremes of pain (the cruel, the bestial, the unnatural), extreme pleasure is incomplete. Once we are into sadism and masochism, vampirism and diabolism, the road is all downhill to necrophilia, coprophilia, transvestism, and the gamut of kinky attitudes laid out by baron von Krafft-Ebing. To the cool, classifying eye of the neurologist, there's nothing inherently ugly, any more than there's anything inherently immoral, in these various practices. But, taken as they were, as adventures in evil, they led directly to exploitation and exaltation of the ugly. It was the adventure of Dorian Gray's rather superficial and moralistic life that esthetic extremes led to extremes of pain, vice, and ugliness. Subtler Des Esseintes, with his long-drawn-out martyrdom on the rack of pleasure, was simply extending and varying the theme. With Zola we move into a world of unrelieved yet somehow grandiose ugliness; later realists diminish the scale but intensify the squalor. As we come toward the modern world, we find Samuel Beckett stripping down the machinery and expanding the implications of his vision, till we have something like a parable without an episode. The nineteenth-century attitude toward the ugly, like the nineteenth-century attitude toward evil, made of it a momentary adventure, a brief plunge from some safe and still recoverable heights. For the protagonist of *How It Is* there is no frame, no perspective, no contrast, no beginning, and no prospect of an end. There is pain, monotony, grief, and just enough helpless striving to ensure neverending frustration.

When Flaubert was writing *Madame Bovary,* the scene in which Charles makes a hideous botch of curing Hippolyte's clubfoot, and is finally forced to amputate the entire leg, was one over which he worked long and carefully. It was a special and precious effect in the texture; Flaubert wove it artfully in among the various tonalities of the novel, so it would stand out as a fulcrum for Emma's feelings about her husband, and

reverberate against Homais' eternal homilies on progress and self-improvement. Delighted with its effec-
tiveness, the next generation of novelists busied themselves with the device, each man fabricating his own
"Hippolyte's leg" for his own romance. But when
novels came to consist almost entirely of Hippolyte's
leg, the neutering of the effect could not be far away. A
modern novelist sometimes drops shit on his page or
signals to his reader with a putrescent canker-sore, as
languidly as he displays a credit card, and without pro-
ducing much more of a sensation. I'm not talking
about Samuel Beckett here, just about an inflation of
the symbols of the ugly, caused by an oversupply—
and Beckett is one of the authors of that oversupply.

A great deal of ugly is associated with our own animal functions. It is an act of self-consciousness quite
distinct from the act of self-forgetfulness that constitutes the classic response to beauty. Engorging, digest-
ing, and excreting are what the ugly often brings to
mind; they are aspects of our daily selves that we want
to, and perhaps have to, suppress. Associated with this
are feelings about an exoskeletal structure, as in snails,
bugs, crabs, and imaginary monsters, of which we are
conscious as crusty on the outside and mushy on the
inside. Dragons and fearful beasts, such as Saint
George is constantly impaling or Perseus relentlessly
smiting, generally have scales, claws, fangs, beaks, and
the horny carapaces of outsize insects. Reversal of
magnitude is at work here, along with an inside-

outside reversal that leads to an ugly tinged with help-less fascination. Nature, we feel, is being turned upside down, inside out, back to front, with incompatible elements in irrational combination. On another level, Bosch and Breughel, those masters of the grotesque and macabre, are fond of working eggs into their pic-tures—generally cracked or open eggs, often with the minimal features and appendages to make them look like human heads. In itself, the egg is an elegant and cleanly spheroid; in a human context, it reminds us of that part of our anatomy where we too are exoskeletal —where, if you crack the outer shell, you will spill out an ugly grey mass of shapeless paste, within which filthy ideas germinate and fester. Hardshell creatures seem to have a close link with the ugly, not only be-cause they threaten to crack us open with claws and pincers, but because when they themselves are cracked open, they image forth some part of us.

Surely the ugly is rooted in fear (not excluding fear of ourselves), as the beautiful is rooted in lust; only it has departed less decisively from its primitive roots. "Esthetic distance" has imposed itself on our ideas of the beautiful, idealizing, spiritualizing, intellectualiz-ing them, and in the process largely purging them of elements once native to them, elements of physical pleasure and direct sensual gratification. With the ugly, less purification of this sort has taken place; the concept retains most of its instinctual, gut implications. For this difference Plato and the Renaissance Platonizers, who wrote so much about beauty and so little about the ugly, may bear some special responsibility; but the whole structure of Christian values, with their emphasis on the spiritual and immaterial, tends to identify beauty with the universal or abstract, even the geometrical or mathematical, while associating the ugly with the particular, the expressive, and the material. An overhang from this sort of idealism shadows Herr Rosenkranz, who thinks our world (which, unhappily, he had not seen) would be beautiful if it were a perfect geometrical sphere. Because, instead, it is flattened a bit at the poles and afflicted with mountains and valleys which give it a deplorable irregularity, he declares it ugly. Like his master Hegel, Rosenkranz was evidently unlucky in cosmic speculations, as well as simplistic in his esthetic ideals.

Though almost nobody anymore thinks the beautiful is to be identified simply with the geometrical, a principle of harmony is clearly a major component, and all sorts of mathematical formulas have been devised to capture the essence. Pythagoras had his harmonious proportions, Hogarth his "line of beauty," and Fibonacci's ratio is perhaps more persuasive than either. Fortunately, none of these beauty-formulas has so far proved more than suggestive; in any event, the formula, if one could be found, would be self-destroying, since multiplication of identical patterns would lead, inevitably, to monotony and disgust. Perhaps because it's less self-regarding, more evocative and various in its appeal to our sympathies, the beautiful elicits from us a wider range of responses than the ugly. We lose ourselves in the beautiful (the terminology of self-obliteration lies thick around high esthetic experiences), while the ugly throws us back on ourselves. We reject the really ugly, or undergo sensations like horror and disgust that make us aware of ourselves. And perhaps this is why the ugly is commonly a violent shock-sensation; memories of it may haunt a viewer in spite of himself, and then the terminology will be drawn from obsession and incubism, but some element of violation is I think inevitable. Thus it's arguable that an artist of distinction never makes anything ugly all the way through—that, if only in his styling and ordering of the subject, some element of distinction and intelligence will remain, as a corolla around his ugly or a light interfusing it. The monsters that rage and claw at Saint Anthony in Grunewald's famous Issenheim retable are no less illumined by divine radiance than his figure of the risen Christ. Ultimate ugly is a mass of negations—gray, shapeless, torpid, flaccid, self-absorbed, squirming and yawning and scratching and waiting for time to pass. Not a gleam of intelligence redeems it, not a glimpse of self-awareness, not a glimmer of intention or direction.

Obviously, there is no place in the world where, if you search through the sewers and watch vigilantly at the slaughter-houses, you won't be confronted with a good deal of ugliness and filth. And the habit of nosing it out, with that deep relish of disgust which might be called the *Mondo-Cane* syndrome can confer, even on the supremely loathsome and nauseating, the glitter of a discovery. But apart from what one brings to it, ultimate ugly is in some way global and oppressive; it doesn't simply repeat a single element, but has a quality of infinite variation without change that lays a weight on the heart. The novels of Theodore Dreiser, Marxist political rhetoric, the landscape of northern New Jersey, souvenir shops in airports—these have the special qualities of an ugly which is at once settled into itself, varied in its particulars, yet bound to go on and on interminably.

It would be ridiculous to exclude from a discussion of the increasing autonomy of the ugly the possibility that the world really is getting uglier from year to year. People on the average and in large aggregates tend to be pretty ugly, there are more of them than ever before, the ideologies encourage them to think well of themselves, therefore to expatiate largely (under the rubric "as long as you're comfortable"), and technology makes it necessary for them to work in hives (Tokyo, London, Chicago) while enabling them to cluster in standardized resort-colonies (Waikiki, Miami, the Riviera). Mass production of basics like steel, petrochemicals, rubber, and cement—not to speak of mass waste-disposal—doesn't seem conceivable without a certain amount of deliberate squalor. Civilization rises out of a mound of garbage, into which it is continually subsiding. But in this flashy, fashionable observation, it seems clear, an attitude is expressed, rather than a set of facts. Man has been excreting and polluting for a good while now: much modern awareness of this distressing condition seems forced and *voulu*. We wouldn't emphasize civilization as an affair of tatters and dreck if we hadn't first decided that we ourselves are compounded of tatters and dreck—that laying claim to this inauthentic and corrupt status is the most authentic option open to us.

Thus, if shit—the word, the substance, and the self-corruption that both symbolize—has domesticated itself at the center of our cultural consciousness, it's partly because the world *is* befouling itself at an amazing rate. But it's also partly as a kind of bad-faith way of establishing good faith. We talk blatantly about what has traditionally been unmentionable to show that we are above the genteel conventions. The once-unspeakable word is a shorthand display of how genuine we are, how free of the suffocating influences, how *real*. The whole Honest-John caper is as devious and as self-frustrating as the parable of the Cretan liar.

Still, if one lets the enthymeme pass, and it's too general to be challenged, ugly instantly becomes beautiful, because it is true. The scandalous proposition of Keats's urn, about the identity of beauty and truth, is fulfilled by being stood on its head. The opposite of the triad ugly-beautiful-true is then "plastic," a word summarizing qualities of glossy fraud and vacant pretension found, for example, in Holiday Inns, urban-renewal projects, Disney movies, and nineteenth-century mortuary sculpture. "Plastic" joins "ugly" with "beautiful" by constituting itself the opposite of both and accepting the onus of fraud as well. This particular twist of terminology is perhaps too cute to last long; but it has at least the virtue of distinguishing varnished ugly, or whited-sepulchre ugly, from a frank and manly ugly—Lincoln-ugly, which is, in its own way, beautiful.

Any art that consists primarily of assault is bound to rely heavily on the ugly, beauty being traditionally committed (as Edmund Burke said long ago) to ingratiation, even seduction. In artfully positioned spots (as when that slimy, goggling monster is dragged out of the sea to reflect Marcello to himself, at the end of *La Dolce Vita*), the shock exactly completes and summarizes the preceding human developments. That shock-effects can be sustained, or repeated at close intervals, is less clear. Even movies, which, with their special command over space and time, can present the horrible and the obscene in strobe-light flashes of perception, seem to spot them fairly carefully, and as much for fear of monotony as of the censor. Even here, though, Rosenkranz's dialectical antithesis between beauty and ugly is *mal à propos,* for both are extremes of perception, and hardly any work of art fails to build its main contrasts out of less pointed opposites.

As we commonly use the terms, it seems unlikely that either "ugly" or "beautiful" would feel natural as applied to the writings of Barth, Malamud, or Pinter, the art-work of DeKooning, Pollock, or Henry Moore. With some more historical perspective on the problem, we may someday come to see the beautiful-ugly antithesis as one more stage in the disintegration of the old division between high, low, and middle styles. That division, which separated not only styles but character-types and literary genres, according to their relative degrees of "nobility," went out with the hierarchical society of which it was an emblem. Perhaps the ugly-beautiful dichotomy should go with it, as a fundamentally exterior division. Seen from the inside, or at least with an attempt to conceive that inside image, the deformed and lonely freak is a rebuke to our complacent and superficial cruelties, if not a lightning-rod for the sacred. Carson McCullers and Flannery O'Connor come immediately to mind as writers who have given this half-pathetic turn to the ugly, and Beckett has not been above it.

The fact is that though most shock-art depends on some form of ugly, not all ugly is shock-art. Medieval dances of death were admonitory and didactic, medieval gargoyles derisively and joyously obscene. The loathly lady in the Wyf of Bath's tale represents a courtesy-test to be faced, and the hideous carl who passes through *Aucassin and Nicolette* in search of his lost ox Roget, the best of his team, seems to say to that fantastic, sentimental little romance, "I'll show you what *real* troubles are." For Apuleius the ugly ass is but a metaphor of our larval stage in this earthly life, to be transcended by eating the roses of Isis; for Kafka, the roach is a prison-house of self-loathing to which Gregor Samsa is suddenly, permanently, and in the end fatally condemned. The distinct but cogent uglinesses of Orwell's *1984* and Huxley's *Brave New World* are set directly against the positive Utopias of the late nineteenth century, such as Morris's *News from Nowhere* and Bellamy's *Looking Backward.* It is not easy to say whether *Last Exit to Brooklyn* represents an advance on the *Satyricon* of Petronius, and if so, in what direction. We recall Karl Shapiro's poem on the fly ("Oh, hideous little bat, the size of snot"), with its sharp, lyric cry, yet this is but a child's naughty game, compared with the distorted rhetorical rage of Dylan Thomas's *"Holy" Sonnets.* Ben Jonson's poem "On the Famous Voyage" is a deliberate adventure in the fecal, as smeary and slimy as any poem could possible be, but it is funny as well as disgusting—somehow, its unbuttoned high spirits take a lot of the edge off its ugly. The ugly can be not only an end but a bottom. When we go to a movie by Bergmann, and find in the first reel or two a couple of people behaving quietly and considerately to one another, we know with a death-and-taxes assurance that this is all contrived and corrupt, that before long they will be shrieking, weeping, punching one another up, and throwing the crockery about—thereby revealing aspects of their personality that must be genuine because they are so ugly. But the movies have so largely domesticated themselves in the hideous and the harrowing, that documenting the range and scope of their endeavors—from *Last Tango* and *Chinatown,* through disaster and catastrophe flicks galore, to *The Exorcist* and *Jaws*—would surely be superfluous. Shock and scare effects come natural to the medium, and have been its stock in trade since Lon Chaney and beyond. More recent extensions of the ugly can be documented in the paintings of Francis Bacon, in an opera like *Bomarzo,* in gallows humor and macabre cartoons so frequent and so widely distributed that they're the unquestioned texture of our existence.

As Gulliver found out in Brobdingnag, the difference between ugly and beautiful may often be simply an angle of vision or a difference of distance; the point can be verified, without any need of sixty-foot maids in waiting, by looking closely at the blobs of pigment on an Impressionist canvas, and watching them melt into a finished image as our point of view recedes. The story is too old to need emphasis that some uglies are merely momentary unfamiliars. To eighteenth-century ears, Mozart's Quartet K. 465 was so grating that it was named "The Dissonant"; ears hardened to post-Schoenberg dissonances will find it hard to imagine why. After the event (the event being simply the persuasive success of the new style), it is easy to relish the folly of those who objected to the discords of Eliot's poetry or Stravinsky's music as ugly and inexpressive. Yet there's another cant to the question, because the domestication of these cultural objects has evidently been the product as much of habit as of understanding. We now know the *Sacré du printemps,* we know *The Waste Land;* as we experience them again and again, the parts are always just where they used to be, and we take their juxtaposition for granted. Perhaps the first critics, who experienced the full shock of these contrasts and discords, have something to tell us about them that our better "understanding" has obscured.

Custom generally softens the ugly, and not only in the sense of making the homely familiar, therefore endearing. The human mind is very agile. We read in *Spectator* 17 of an Ugly Club, which implies the conversion of a disability to a privilege. One imagines the members sitting in judgment on a candidate for admission: "No, he's ugly, he's *very* ugly; but ugly enough to be one of us, that he's not." Particular forms of ugly may be barnacled over with a rich crust of by-no-means-unpleasant associations. What baseball player has been more affectionately admired, of recent years, than Yogi Berra? The admiration might have come for his skill at the game; the affection welled up in response to his uncouth diction, combined with his really imposing ugliness. We dislike automatically the person too conscious of his-or-her own beauty; from Cyrano de Bergerac to Alex Karras, we respond sympathetically to the person who mocks his own ugliness. The small-town New England protestantism of my largely untheological youth brings to mind oyster-yellow or cabbage-green stained glass, along with wailing, half-hearted psalm-singing. Ugly so ungainly and awkward was human and endearing; I should have been overawed by the Parthenon or the cathedral at Chartres, but the First Congregational Church was just ugly enough to be comfortable.

Whether ugly thus frosted over with affection is still really ugly remains a question for metaphysical estheticians. It certainly points up an intimacy between pleasure and the ugly that could be documented in a variety of contexts. Like any other quality, when it's spectacular and outstanding the ugly yields a sort of delighted surprise: "Did you ever see anything as ugly as *that*?" When in some special sense it's ours, we can be proud of it. Nelson Algren compares living in Chicago to sleeping with a woman with a broken nose; those of us unlucky enough to have missed that delectable experience can only surmise how real it must be. Some people—present company always excepted—like to think of themselves as connoisseurs of the ugly; and for some, it's a counter in the game of advantage, when by refusing some tawdry prettiness one establishes, before others and oneself, a more severe and authentic stance.

All these instances add up to no more than an assertion that judgments of the ugly, like esthetic judgments in general, are caught up in the workings of the personal psyche. If there's anything special about them, it's only that they tend to be a little more inward and self-regarding, as well as more violent, and so drag up with them, perhaps, a little more psychic flotsam and jetsam than do our judgments of the agreeable, the delightful, and the admirable. The new (or re-newed) personalist criticism may well be a perfectly appropriate response to a kind of confrontation-art, one of whose main vehicles is the repellent.

What a mnice old mness it all mnakes!
A middenhide hoard of objects! Olives, beets,
kimmells, dollies, alfrids, beatties,
cormacks and daltons.
Finnegans Wake

Rags, Garbage, and Fantasy

If elegance and dignity are qualities of the spirit, then rags and garbage are the natural habitat of the aristo-rat. He does not repose in them as a child in nature, but accepts them as a test, the ineluctable antagonist of his instinctive style. You may recognize a princess by her sensitivity to a single pea under a mountain of mat-tresses; with equal assurance you may recognize a prince by the way he arranged his few filthy rags, by he way he carries a drooping daisy plucked from a dunghill, by the port (neither jocose nor disconsolate) of his skeletal umbrella on a sunshine day.

The best-bred display of breeding is made with min-imal expense and, more importantly, with minimal effort. The two requirements are by no means equiva-lent. A celebrated Japanese tea-master remarked one particular gate in the shogun's garden as a false note; it was, he declared, a little too rude and rustic, slightly pretentious in its blatant humility. A worthy tea-master! a sensitive shogun! He altered at once the comportment of the offending gate. When truly and naturally poverty-stricken, the dandy is liable to no such charge. Since his rags are worn by necessity, not choice, only the form he imposes on them is his responsibility. He is thus a central figure for this bedraggled twentieth century, when even nature appears second-hand and contrived, and all mankind flaunts tatters made of yesterday's rags as it sinks steadily into an accumulation of today's garbage. If man was ever nature's child, he is so no longer; on the contrary, in an Oedipal violation of colossal proportions, he is either the murderer of nature or its guardian. Even the natural is now man-made, man-protected, man-controlled. Whales, once emblems of a fierce and cruel universe, beyond man's wildest power to strike, have become the objects of a protective campaign; and the once-divine power to impart or withhold life is crudely manipulated by pressure groups—never more fitly so called. Whether we now see the city as a refuge from the idiocy of rural life, or the natural existence as an escape from urban uproar, we live always among castoffs and leftovers, on which the mark of some social and practical decision is still legible.

Rags and garbage, particular stages in never-ending cycles, are nothing but materials momentarily exhausted of their value by human wear or consumption. The polite name for garbage, "refuse," carries the crucial concept of human rejection. Second-hand clothing bears the implication that it wasn't good enough for someone else, but for the unfortunate without any self-respect it may, even as contaminated by the first owner, still be good enough. Garbage, as what someone has refused to eat, wears even more openly the imprint of the rejected. "Sheol," the Hebrew word for "hell," originally meant simply the garbage-dump of Jerusalem. Scavengers of all sorts are stigmatized as unclean. "Dog" and "pig" become terms of ultimate insult, and garbagemen, who simply carry the stuff away, are objects of avoidance; in India, they find themselves segregated into a pariah caste. The word "pariah," deriving from "drum," is itself an avoidance-word at second hand: the caste which it designates carried refuse and cleaned streets, but became known euphemistically by the most reputable of its occupations, the beating of the village drum. A British equivalent is the word "dustman" for a man who will pick up dust, indeed, if it is put out for him, but who is mostly concerned with what OED nicely refers to as "&c."

Nature then, even nature, wears man's smudge and shares man's smell—in harsh and horrible reality manywheres, but most of all in the depths of the living imagination. Even if the garbage-piles are split-second stages in nature's progress toward forests primeval, and the mountains of waste mere pimples on the rise and fall of slightly more substantial hills—even in a Grand-Canyon perspective of time—we can hardly help feeling the cycles to be in their rubbish-phase now. The feeling may even be right, but we entertain it in good part for reasons other than material evidence, reasons which exercise their own necessity upon us.

Schliemann, digging ruthlessly through the rubble of nine or sixteen or twenty-three successive Troys in search of Homer's (it was actually amid the first junk he mingled contemptuously with other "modern" Troys and threw aside), demonstrated better than he ever realized how history heaps one trashpile atop another. History does not unfold: it piles up and is dug out. The first and most wonderful of books, the Egyptian *Book of the Dead* (of which *Finnegans Wake* is so lavish an imitation), tells us that its lore is immemorial, the entire book having been written by the god Thoth, in whose divine nature all the thousands of scribes and copyists who produced the millions of potsherds and papyrus scraps in which the *Book* subsists, directly participated. This earliest book explicitly declares and rejoices in the antiquity of its wisdom, which is smeared and smelly with mansmell, *therefore* divine; and it celebrates all chaotic fragmentation as the work of a supernal and lucid intelligence. From these ancient perspectives, our sense that the modern world is exhausted and falling into squalor is not, indeed, negated; but it is qualified, as merely one of several styles of feeling. We may actually, in our disappointment with the enlightenment myth, be falling victim to it—our dismay with the bloody mess of history rising from unacknowledged springs of expectation that history can or should be a tidy, sanitary process. Human rags and garbage are then the special badges of our shame, evidence of our willful refusal to be clean, rational, and proper, as we easily could be if we followed our better natures. This is a defensible point of view, maybe, but it is not inevitable.

The last age to be interested in rags as such (not as momentary badges of oppression or vagabond freedom, but as ingredients of style) was the eighteenth century. The Newgate pastoral that Swift proposed to Gay held up before its audience a two-way distorting mirror—reflecting on the one hand the plight of the modern swain (dispossessed, exiled from his native soil, and chivvied into urban slums), on the other hand the state of modern society and government (the overworld), where thievery is organized as methodically as in the underworld. Pickpockets and prostitutes exchange with lords and ladies the compliment of reciprocal imitation; and the stolen rags of a drab thus stand for a whole system of dignities and emoluments filched from the now-destitute Stuarts by the House of Hanover, as well as for a whole system of violated nature and ruined shepherdesses. Implications are made explicit in names: Macheath is a Scot, for instance, therefore probably a clansman, an outlaw, and a Jacobite. (These are all ingredients of high style: he is not a pauper but a laird, not a thief but a soldier of the nation's rightful king, and what he wears is not a rag but the tartan plaid of an ancient and honorable clan.) In passing, we note further that Macheath is also a child of the unenclosed common, one of nature's noblemen;

and his name chimes on that of Macbeth, a fellow Scot who tried to usurp a kingdom and failed through a weakness before women. The rags of the felons before us serve to diminish the larger actions which they shadow; the echo-actions serve equally to dignify and render heroic the criminals. The play consists simply of seeing these parallels and doing nothing about them, as it makes perfectly clear by exploding its own human consequences in the farcical ending. Rags are a powerful image throughout the performance; they dominate Gay's action by the sheer insistence of their presence. But the fact that men in rags instinctively duplicate the patterns of men in ribbons solidifies those patterns, rooting them in slum dirt as straight pastoral would have rooted them in the soil of nature.

By contrast, the Brecht-Weill adaptation of Gay's burlesque as "The Three-Penny Opera" is loaded with Marxist, i.e., millennial, social commentary and expectation. The rags worn by highwaymen and pickpockets are a proletarian uniform, wrongfully imposed on them by a social order which can and will be changed. No particular joke is possible about the interchangeable fine manners of gentlemen and highwaymen, because there are no visible gentlemen, and if there were, they would be moral inferiors of the thieves. Peachum and Lockit, representing bourgeois morality, are the loftiest social class in view, and the lessons emerge (1) that bosses are greedy, (2) that proles would be good as gold if allowed to make a clean sweep of bosses, and (3) that rags, while em-

Rags, Garbage, and Fantasy

blems of present oppression, promise liberation and revenge in the future. The two versions differ as comedy differs from didactic melodrama.

Swift himself, in his first full-scale satire, not only made use of rags as the emblem of modern style in philosophy, religion, and authorship; he became one of the first writers actually to construct a whole book out of verbal tatters. Diderot, Sterne, Flaubert, and Joyce are among his followers. A major point of *A Tale of a Tub* is that it consists of appendages and appurtenances, posturings and apologies, decorations and extranea, overwhelming a notable deficiency of central structure. The comic device is not anything Swift could have learned from Rabelais, Lucian, or Scarron; it depends on a self-conscious and contemptuous view of the modern age as contrasted with the ancients, which converts self-derision into a vehicle of historical criticism. Because modern men (including most notably the author of the *Tale*) are degenerate, they exist in moral and intellectual rags; if they chose to be whole of mind and simple of spirit, they might still emulate ancient magnanimity, under the guidance of Sir William Temple. But they are incapable of that choice. Far from being an accident or an imposition, rags represent a permanent spiritual state.

As the example suggests, rags are always controlled, like other literary props, by a context; what they can be made to mean is elastic and various. Dutch genre painters, of whom the elder Pieter Breughel is one of the first and surely the greatest, seem to accept a high degree of raggedness as normal in their models. Breughel himself certainly lived among and worked for people who were far from ragged, but for reasons at which we can only guess, they liked to look at grotesquely tattered figures in their paintings. Whatever Breughel himself felt about the filth and squalor he customarily portrays, his boors are commonly in rags, and his sales to men of wealth and distinction did not suffer. Commentators, rendered uneasy by so much routine frowziness in his world, tend to edge up on it under a bristle of rhetorical questions. "Is it possible that . . . ?" or "May it not well be that . . . ?" Their uncertainty contrasts with the immediate import of rags in novels by Defoe *(Colonel Jack, Moll Flanders)* or Dickens *(Oliver Twist, Our Mutual Friend)*. Like the dirt and squalor portrayed by Hogarth and Doré in their representations of London, rags are here the objects of finely focussed and quite unequivocal feelings.

Wearing rags, but wearing them with a deliberate difference, like clowns or mimes, is a way of rising above circumstance by style, a device of levitation that divides the world into horizontal levels and thereby negates any need for temporal or vertical advancement. If the nadir of misery can be transformed by a knack of gesture or expression into laughter, applause, and pots of money, then the way up and the way down are indeed one and the same; and there's no occasion to climb any visible or invisible ladder. The best way to rise is by falling; and this paradigm has had many applications off the formal stage, as well as on. Within our own time, rags have had a widespread vogue among the young, partly as protest against straight society, partly from a sense that being grubby is a way to be natural and therefore perhaps next thing to holy. When a snake-dance of such types invaded a graduation ceremony I was attending, they wore very ragged rags indeed, and a bare minimum of those—rags supplemented only euphemistically by paint and hair, to suggest, I suppose, that the agents existed above and below civilized forms. Drugs would naturally encourage this sort of display, as on the particular occasion they did; but so would any strong *other*-experience. Living in a different world, sensual, imaginary, and presumably better, the addict advertises by costume or behavior his contempt for this common and commonplace globe. Rags easily serve such an end; so, though with very different accent and feeling, the hermits of the Thebaid, or Saint Simeon Stylites and his ilk, cultivated rags and filth as a way to express their loathing of fleshly lusts and the world that caters to them. In thus acting out a disdain for middle-class decorums, rags may express an aloofness almost *dandy* in its sense of extreme style.

Especially nowadays, when shopgirls and countesses are masquerading as something equally remote from them both (whether whore or pre-pubescent), when movie actors are hard put to outshine shoe-salesmen, copping out of the competition by opting for rags is an obvious one-up alternative. It carries the special escape-mechanism that on the face of things one isn't trying, really trying, at all. The pre-tattered Brooks Brothers sport jacket, the Peck and Peck dress which is called, and is, "just a rag I threw on," but is visibly a Peck and Peck rag—these represent a highly contrived strategy for having it both ways.

To the serious taste of our age, second-hand may really be better than first: less pretentious, more authentic, richer in patina, more revealing of true gust. The principle is perhaps akin to that which declares bastards lustier and more vigorous than legitimate scions, because the offspring of pleasure, not obligation. So, when not encumbered by any dynastic obligations and pretensions to high "originality," artistic work may be freer, more vital. Whether formed on these principles or not, the vogue is widespread for collages, *objets trouvés,* and mechanically multiplied images, all of which have in common a quality of playing down the uniqueness and originality of the art work. To pick something out of a junk heap or off a street corner and place it on a pedestal shows (or so we are to suppose) greater acuteness than creating after an imaginary model of one's own. The effect is obtained with minimum effort; it is shared in a specially intimate bond between artist and viewer as almost co-creators. On both parts, it implies a purer act of intellection, in seeing through a perceptible barrier of unfamiliarity to a shape which is new only because of a common act of eye and mind. Like rags and castoffs generally, second-hand materials are of preference for a thoroughly modern artist. They bear open witness to what scholarship is constantly reminding us, that we never observe objects with totally fresh, i.e., unprepared eyes. Since the experience is already contaminated by the viewer's expectations (themselves structured by his culture, his tradition, his prior definition of an art-object), the frank thing to do is to make unconcealed use of those expectations by crossing them up and doubling them back.

Thus Joyce, Eliot, and Pound, when they set about creating a literature of modernism, unanimously turned to a texture, if not a structure, of tags, allusions, quotations, misquotations, and phrases at second hand. What Eliot's personage calls "fragments shored against my ruin" are for Joyce and Pound the very stuff of history and psychology, the depth and movement of which are only to be measured by matching fragment with fragment. By patching together the rags of fable, folklore, and fiction, the writer in this vein may hope to suggest the seamless garment of total history, or some image of it. He readily avoids the appearance of preaching, and makes tangible use of the past as something more than the merely picturesque. For visibly second-hand materials inevitably create ironic duplicity, because the object is seen simultaneously in two contexts, with a third meaning materializing wraith-like out of the distance or difference between them. How that third meaning actually comes out matters less, perhaps, than that past and present have conspired in making it. An inherently eclectic age like our own, aware of several pasts in almost every present act, self-conscious and thought-bound like Prufrock, could hardly find a more appropriate style.

Bloom, as Everyman, is of particular interest. Physically, he is a neat and cleanly Jew in a city of dirty Christians, yet he has dealt in old clothes and is mocked with the nickname "Ole Clo." His fondness for the well-worn and smudgy phrase is reinforced by his evident wish to have a well-worn and smudged wife. One of the many reasons why he is Jewish is that ancient history lives on in him past the term of its meaning; he is a fouled well of thought. Like his memories, his aspirations are compounded of clichés and formulas jumbled indiscriminately together. In the eyes of Dublin, he is a used, discounted, and despised article, invariably put aside or set down with a phrase of disparagement. As a creature of flesh, blood, and thought, he is nearly as scruffy as his sometimes-nauseous wife. But in their differing degrees—she more than he—both are transparent vessels of something else, containers of a truth and vision to which they themselves are nearly blind. This vision has nothing to do with the conscious mind, whose scraps and counters Stephen Dedalus manipulates with the virtuosity, and often with the obtuseness, of a highly trained graduate student. In their differing degrees—Stephen more than Bloom—both are ragged men, nearly as hollow and disintegrated as Eliot's straw dummies. But Molly as Maya the weaver (Calypso,

Circe, and Penelope, all weavers, are her avatars) will incorporate them and all men into her pattern. If anyone can, she will make whole cloth of their tatters.

Looking at *Ulysses* across this schema is probably good for *Ulysses;* it gets us out of some sentimental hangups about Bloom and Molly, and gives weight to the end of the novel, where weight has often seemed to be wanting. But it also leads us directly into *Finnegans Wake,* where it always helps to arrive with a sense of one's preliminary bearings. Of course if one thinks *Finnegans Wake* an eccentric venture off the main path of modern perception and expression, then the fact that it is deeply involved with rags and garbage won't make much difference. But if one sees it as centrally involved with rags and garbage, that may constitute an argument that it's at the center of modern problems of perception and expression.

In the first place, it must be clear that the book is not much concerned with "characters," that is, with human nature; nor, consequently, with manners or morals, both of which topics predicate an individual identity. Because they are not properly individuals, but rather silhouettes and recurrent verbal patterns, the personages of the *Wake* exist freely at several widely removed periods of time, under widely differing physical forms—animal, human, vegetable, mineral, geographical, mythical, and religious, to name only a few. Their nature at any particular moment of the book, and their connections with their multiple analogues, are suggested by recurrent verbal tags and formulas.

Like Schliemann, the digger into the *Wake* must always be guessing from bits and scraps of evidence what level he's at. His efforts are mimicked and encouraged at the same time by the story of a hen, Biddy Doran, who, apart from being a manifestation of ALP, may also be a phoenix or a barnacle goose. She is trying to decipher a letter (*The Book of the Dead, Finnegans Wake,* an ancient Irish inscription, any historical document) which she has found on a dunghill (the gravemound at Heliopolis, the delta of the Liffey at Dublin-Healyopolis, any tumulus of any buried culture). What she has to go on are henscratches, of course, but also stains, rips, blurs, and smudges in the original document—plus potsherds, marrowbones, junk, and coprolites from the circumadjacent dunghill. Reading the *Wake* is reading the claybook of the earth itself, reading the record of history, reading the structure of human character—all of which are alike and equally piles of tattered and miscellaneous garbage through which the blurred outlines of an intricate design can perhaps be perceived.

Doublespeech in all its various forms is the natural language of this sort of vision. Puns, palindromes, anagrams, and acrostics abound, along with citations, parodies, symbols, metaphors both buried and exploded, and those nameless misspellings which evoke from a familiar word unfamiliar, semi-relevant components and long-muted voices. Syntax serves an expressive-depressive end by choking and stammering over an excess of jumbled, jostling meanings; and

lists proliferate wildly—lists overt and subsurface, lists
relevant and irrelevant, lists simultaneously stuffed
with detail and apparently vacant of significance. Like
history's garbage pile, the list is theoretically endless.
The 800 rivers of Anna Livia could just as well flow on
toward 8,000 or ∞. For whatever evidence one assem-
bles toward the full story (which is all stories but also
just one story), however subtly one interrogates and
interprets the fragments, any selection of evidence is
equivalent to any other selection, and all evidence is
inadequate.

The *Wake*, which deliberately derives its materials
from the commonest of sources—patches, clichés,
nursery rhymes, proverbs, stock formulas, slogans,
and verbal refuse—deliberately takes as its central
theme the prospect of resurrection. Finnegan lying
dead at his wake is Finnegan about to wake up; dead as
canned salmon, he is renewed as his offspring sit down
to the family feast and joyously devour him. "Gram-
pupus is fallen down, but grinny sprids the boord."
Probably nobody else could have accomplished it, but
the wedding that Joyce celebrates in *Finnegans Wake*
between the grim and the hilarious, the foul and the
sacred, comes close to a full artistic sacrament. The joy
is, indeed, somewhat scraped up; by the time he was
done with it, Joyce seems to have felt the book as an
incubus, and so it can be for the reader who, as he
reads, feels his mind harrowed by a revolution more
permanent than anything envisioned by Chairman
Mao. The *Wake* is a paradigm for the artist of our

times: a deploring and a celebration, a cathedral built of scraps.

Garbage and carrion, as they remind us intimately of our own imminent corruption, raise more painful feelings than rags, and are the object of deeper, more intricate taboos. They are closer to the sacred, closer to the accursed, because nearer to organic as against artificial process. (For a long time, "garbage" retained its original meaning of guts, entrails; Professor Skeat records a 1530 usage, "garbage of a fowl.") Disintegration and decay are almost the essence of garbage; the basic emotional assumption is that it's all excrement. But our feelings on this subject are themselves curiously tangled. When it's called "compost" or "humus," garbage takes on immediate overtones of life-giving natural process. Cow- and sheep-manure, guano, and rotted vegetable matter are the materials of so-called "organic" farming, healthful and by implication ennobling; chemical fertilizers are the antithetical, "plastic" materials. But what is euphemistically called "night-soil," though perfectly acceptable fertilizer in large areas of the world, is not so in the germ-conscious West.

Scavengers are considered loathsome, but not uniformly so; the rule, illogical as it appears, may run something like, "The bigger and more public, the more repulsive." Buzzards, hyenas, coyotes, rats, roaches, and down to maggot-flies have maintained a generally bad press; but ants are relatively well thought of, as cleanly and industrious creatures (they scavenge chiefly the remains of small animals), and worms are accepted because they do their work decently under ground. The eclectic Egyptians included a jackal in their pantheon along with an alligator, and saw a sacred symbolism in the operations of the scarab or dung-beetle. Bacteria, which are such convenient and manageable scavengers, we tend to look on as friends to man, particularly admirable because they can be constrained or induced to do most of their work invisibly.

Human excrement itself is a learned dislike, therefore a source of guilty pleasure, even, occasionally, an emblem of social freedom or rebellion. Very young children are quite proud of what they can produce, and many "uncivilized" cultures (by which we generally mean no more than cultures with standards different from our own) look upon it with amusement or indifference, not antipathy. Under our conventions, talking about shit openly or covertly is an act of social and psychic revolt, either bluntly defiant or disguised as comedy. The tradition in literature runs from Rabelais to Sir John Harington to Jonson to Swift to Joyce. Mark Twain as well had a scatological side; it is a quality that seems to crop out under pressure of collision between a strong super-ego and a primitivistic libido. Nowadays, ghetto or gutter speech is often worn as a badge; it implies sympathy with the oppressed and exploited classes, it advertises one's rejection of the old élitisms, one's membership in the new fraternity.

Of course excrement and garbage are automatically

obtrusive topics any time one gets masses of people in one place; if not exclusively urban phenomena, they become prominent in urban circumstances. Under the best of conditions, the megalopolis is only a week away from choking on its own crud; wars or strikes bring the prospect immediately closer. And the fact is that industrial wastes, such as a modern city generates in quantity, are a good deal harder to dispose of than traditional trash, excrement, and offal. A traveller through northern New Jersey, south Chicago, the London suburbs, or the communities peripheral to Milan will not need reminding of the evidence. Slag-piles, ashpits, scrap metal, chemical wastes, and auto-graveyards (plus the smaller but more pervasive detritus of bottles, cans, tires, and indestructible plastics) do not absorb quickly into the natural cycles. They stay on hand, they pile up. There is no way to minimize this sort of thing, even if one wished to; it constitutes a vast and terrifying event. Loose talkers blame it on a profit economy, but it seems just as prevalent where production is for use, or is alleged to be so. If mass populations don't invariably equal mass economy, and mass economy doesn't equal mass squalor, the exception has yet to be established. Still, it's too fresh a topic, rooted too largely in statistics and too little in common experience, to have forced its way deeply into the imaginative consciousness. Creative artists have a way of not living in areas of heavy pollution; their indignation with a garbage-economy may be genuine enough (as during the 1930's all sorts of very serious people sincerely believed in the historic mission of the proletariat), but it's a kind of learned indignation. So far it amounts to ideology rather than lived belief.

The deeper strain of feeling, as it seems to me, is not that we are drowning in our own wastes, but that we are, ourselves, that waste. The overpressure of people is constant. Every day of our lives, we swim against a tide of alien faces, are forced astray by a whirl of oppressive traffic; our sensations, feelings, and ideas, such as they are, would all turn out, if we could bear to analyze them, second-hand at best, or thousandth-hand, if we weren't limited by pathetic ignorance. Seriously to contemplate one's abject personal triteness is probably the most painful act a man can perform: it is no meditation of a casual quarter-hour. Meeting every day, as we do, thousands of identical replicas of ourselves, feeling ourselves numbered and processed, catalogued and regulated by a network of impersonal forces, pressured from outside by opinion-molders and convention-formers, and reduced within by psychological analysts to a bundle of predictable tropisms, we naturally have a sense that our identities have been contaminated if not crushed altogether. To reach what is genuine and individual within ourselves (if such a bedrock exists at all) is a work of immense concentration, most of which is self-impeding and self-frustrating, as when a muscle-bound man must struggle to hang loose. At best, introspection is probably no more than an awkward substitute for the practice of using yourself to some specific end.

More than fifty years ago, José Ortega y Gasset gave a set of talks, since augmented, translated, and reprinted under their original title, *The Dehumanization of Art*. ★ They still read interestingly, but what they describe as an event in itself is likely to strike a modern reader as only the symptom of something larger, the dehumanization of people. What the magnificent, mournful elegies of Samuel Beckett describe is a perishing imagination, the death-throes of a mind reduced from all its other enterprises to the desperate repetition of Descartes' minimal assurance: "I (still) think, therefore I (still) am." That a couple of his personages appear onstage in garbage cans, and another one is named after a piece of excrement has horrified people; but it fascinates them too, compelling their identification. The condition Beckett's characters share (frozen, immobilized, disintegrating, bored to death) appeals to the fantasy of his audiences because they recognize in it a stage of their own decomposition, actual or potential but inevitable. That people are garbage is no more true now than it ever was, but it is easier for everyone to suppose, for reasons of which the social psychologists can inform us at more length, perhaps, than we really need. We must all be conscious of mass populations and the weight imposed on us by a commitment to history that has become more pressing as the world has shrunk. A blood-feud in Africa or Micronesia may at any moment blow up into intercontinental ballistic missiles. The suicidal terrorist, who is

★Tr. W. R. Trask, Princeton University Press, 1972. Originally published by the Revista de Occidente, Madrid, 1925.

such a special feature of our times, declares in his action that the enemy has made him a piece of trash, worthless for any other purpose in the world except explosion against the object of his hatred. Less spectacular but more horrifying to the imagination are the torpid mega-populations of the world—the abandoned waifs of South America, the used fellaheen of Egypt, the native populations of Africa, the inert peasants of Bangladesh and India—who accept without audible protest consignment to a world of filth and disease, gutters and garbage. For the dump-dwellers of Mexico City the world is a gigantic dump, as for the ghastly beggars of Calcutta it is an endless maze baited intermittently with a bit of semi-edible filth. Against this structure of things their imagination can hardly rise in protest; for their sort, things have always been as they are now, and herd-like resignation is inevitable. But throughout the rest of the world, precisely because the victims don't protest, the possibility of things being different is naggingly present, and the silent reproach of such an existence gnaws at the conscience. Hence a pervasive uneasiness with the very idea of literature (and of art in general), as an enterprise undertaken in bad faith, which, if it's to be given any credit at all must somehow establish its own ratings. One way for it to do this is by self-parody—not parody of other books, but of the literary enterprise itself; another is by rooting itself in some form of non-literary language, not subject to the suspicions attached to the esthetic. Both enterprises involve a shredding and tattering of arranged esthetic surfaces, a ripping apart of the very idea of façades.

Why, for example, should Donald Barthelme retell the story of Snow White except that it has been so vulgarized and infantilized as to represent literature in its last stages of decomposition? Why make fun of this story except that it is like all other stories, which are equally silly in the face of a modern Snow White's total ennui, the absolute nullity of the seven modern dwarfs, and our practical assurance that any reasonably intelligent wicked stepmother is bound to prevail over that tailor's dummy, Prince Charming? What is the point of pausing in the middle of the story to administer a multiple-choice, short-answer quiz to the reader, unless to mock the pedantry of literary categories and values? Pausing to give criticism a passing kick breaks the story to bits and leaves character a shambles; but story and character never mattered to begin with.

The outline-character capering through a world of scraps and accidents which the author himself derides as artificial is too familiar as a modern type to need underlining. Queneau calls his persons "silhouettes," Mme. Sarraute reduces hers to "tropisms," Thomas Pynchon labels his protagonist "Stencil," Landolfi and Borges, like Barth and Barthelme, build their stories around named persons who are little more than phantoms or formulas. Insofar as they involve people at all, fictions in this mode make use of dehumanized stick figures with whom calisthenic verbal factorings can be performed—expansion, contraction, distortion, cross–multiplication, miniaturization, transmigration. Behind these capering shadows, curiously omni-present but wholly unavowed, lies the transparent shadow of the author himself, the grammar of whose mind we are constantly conscious of exploring. Be-hind the vaudeville a striptease is in progress; among the tatters being discarded is literature.

All this emphasis on disintegration and decay sounds very gloomy; but in fact rags and garbage, apart from their obvious uses in black humor, provide a soil from which unforced humor can spring. The bourgeois, with his somber, respectable uniform, is the source, God help us, of authentic high seriousness; his precarious middle eminence, demanding that he be 'umble, forbidding him to be vulgar, offers no security for derision or exultation. One has to transcend his innocent interest in being regaled with a rousing yarn, his desire for a safe and wholesome moral lesson, to reach the thin, high air that's fit to breathe. Hardly anybody in real life would opt for destitution as a pre-condition of exultation; but precisely for that reason, it's the business of literature as a surrogate form of experience, to explore the strategies of total loss by forcing us to feel like Lear and Samson, Hamm behind his stancher and Krapp turning off his last tape. It's arguable that our literary fascination with rags springs up when the reading public is comfortably clothed, and that garbage and dung are the natural fixations of a people with the most elaborate sewage-disposal sys-tem since the later Roman empire. How else are we, the reading public in our uneasy easy circumstances, to know destitution, filth, and squalor, unless by an imaginative reading of them? The future may well have a hideous answer to that question, but, even so, Mithridates' strategy seems applicable for the time being.

Some early artists in rags, like those improbable bedfellows, Swift and Piranesi, used them to contrast with the strong integrity of the antique world. For all their hectic elegance, people are the ragged vermin who swarm over Piranesi's ruins, hopelessly diminished by the weight and dignity of the past. Just like Swift's "modern" author, they are so dwarfed and humiliated by the gigantic austerities of antiquity, that nothing is left for them but posture and display. But Alessandro Magnasco, the eighteenth-century Genoese painter, makes no such contrast. He simply saw the world under the aspect of rags and dirt. He saw it that way consistently, all the time. Because his subjects were often fantastic, one doesn't share the happiness or project the sympathy that sometimes surrounds Breughel's boors. Magnasco's contemporaries, Guardi and Tiepolo, share some elements of his style, but never fail to make their paintings more ingratiating. Magnasco renders the world in flitters, and there is no knowing whether he thought it, thus seen, to be funny or horrible or commonplace. It is a completely open question, to which I do not know the answer; I do not know how to find out.

A final contrast illustrates the vast difference that is made by the locus of an artist's ugly. Jacques Callot displays an exuberant delight in the ripped and torn, but he is not buried in it, like Magnasco. He always tips the sordid with the elegant. He can sketch a couple of buffoons, a gaggle of gypsies, a ghastly battlefield, or the confusion and diversity of a great fair, all with the same leaping, energetic line. That independence of any particular subject matter, that superiority of mind to material, is of course what every artist is out to intimate. Callot's gypsies imply a relation to gypsies that goes beyond their ragged surfaces; his etching of "The Fair at Impruneta" implies the full man, whose dignity would not allow him to obey a direct order from Louis XIII because it implied a discourtesy to the prince of his native Lorraine. Rags and the common dirt were Callot's chosen materials, but he never touched them save in cleanliness of spirit.

It is exactly the opposite with Urs Graf, the hateful Swiss. Graf left only a few drawings and woodcuts, plus a single oil painting titled, pointedly "War." It was a subject he knew well and relished deeply. All his artistic work is of the highest quality—bold, energetic, dramatic—yet hardly anything he did fails to have at its center some act of atrocious, and generally gratuitous, cruelty. Saint Catherine, held up by the hair, is about to be decapitated by a burly, saber-wielding soldier; the background is cool, placid, almost vacant, a Swiss mountain lake. Or again, a place of execution is depicted, with wheel and scaffold and the inevitable consequences—a cage of bones, dripping guts, a hungry vulture. Most curious in this woodcut is a sign on a post which can be deciphered to read, "Look out for yourself." One gets a real sense of a surly, sadistic man with his artistic talents somehow on the surface, as opposed to Callot who, for all the horrors he depicted, was gracious and a humorist. Urs Graf, who made his living as a mercenary, died at about the age of forty while participating in the Sack of Rome. It's appropriate that he perished in the greatest orgy of looting, rape, murder, torture, and sheer disorganized savagery that the civilized world had seen since Attila the Hun. It couldn't have happened, as we say, to a nicer guy.

Whether it's on the surface or in the psyche, the ugliness an artist finds or makes or lives is bound to come out, and is easy enough to recognize, enumerate, even to classify. But around it lie psychic strategies of such deviousness, or sometimes of such simplicity and directness, as to baffle language altogether.

If nothing else, the experience of writing categorically about the hateful and negative side of the imagination suggests that the topic requires some leaven of style or perspective. The deeper we sink into the sullen mud of life, the fewer articulate noises we can make about it, unless we lift our faces now and then to the sun. Like a lesion in the mind, really deep ugly-responses easily scab over or fester into self-loathing; the former is better than the latter, neither is very pretty. But as there are many varieties of dark fancy, so there are many opposites and complements; it sometimes even happens that the best palliative of an aching head is a sprained ankle. Robert Burton, anatomizing melancholy three and a half centuries ago, reported sagely that the best cure of the condition was identical with its most frequent cause: study. The slip-slop of documents, the throb of accumulating particulars, the restless rhythm of the hobby-horse are sovereign. Action, action, more and more action. Like pebbles rolling over and over in a tumbler, the samples of ugly that one has accumulated may take on, from one another, a smoother gloss, a deeper luster. Or if that hope is delusive, activity that delays for a while recognition of its own futility may not be altogether futile.